Dyspraxia

Dyspraxia

A Guide for Teachers and Parents

Kate Ripley, Bob Daines, Jenny Barrett

David Fulton Publishers
London

David Fulton Publishers Ltd
Ormond House, 26–27 Boswell Street, London WC1N 3JD

First published in Great Britain by David Fulton Publishers 1997
Reprinted 1997, 1998 (twice) and 1999

British Library Cataloguing in Publication Data
A catalogue record for this book is available from the British Library

ISBN 1–85346–444–9

Typeset by Sheila Knight
Printed in Great Britain by Bell and Bain Ltd, Glasgow

Contents

Acknowledgements   vii

About the Authors   ix

1 What is Dyspraxia?   1

2 Dyspraxia: a Developmental Perspective   8

3 The Assessment of Dyspraxia   13

4 The Development of Voluntary Movement   22
   and How to Help

   4.1 Whole body movement, coordination   25
        and body image

   4.2 Physical play   30

   4.3 Dressing   33

   4.4 Handwriting and drawing   34

   4.5 Speech and language   43

   4.6 Feeding and eating   56

5 Living with Dyspraxia   64

   Appendix   91

   Glossary   93

   Useful addresses   95

   References   97

   Index   99

Acknowledgements

We are indebted to the following colleagues who have helped to shape our thinking over many years and who have made valuable contributions to the final manuscript. Without their advice and assistance we would have been unable to achieve such a balanced perspective.

Maureen Abbott   SENCO for West Hove Junior School, an experienced teacher of children with motor coordination difficulties.

Peter Cartlidge   SENCO and deputy headteacher of Carden Junior School, a pioneer in running motor coordination groups.

Sue Crane   senior specialist speech and language therapist at McKeith Centre, Royal Alexander Children's Hospital, Brighton; specialist in feeding and preschool children with special needs.

Elizabeth Green   consultant neurodevelopmental paediatrician, McKeith Centre; specialist in developmental disorders.

We would like to thank the occupational therapists at the McKeith Centre for their comments on the manuscript. Our thanks also go to Greer Bailey for her patient typing and re-typing of the manuscript.

About the Authors

Kate Ripley is Senior Educational Psychologist for language and communication disorders in Hampshire. Her interest in dyspraxia began while working with speech and language impaired children at two of the I CAN schools and at Moor House. Kate is secretary of NAPLIC (National Association for Professionals Working with Language Impaired Children) and, with Bob Davies, contributes regularly to AFASIC training seminars.

Bob Daines's varied career has covered postgraduate studies, research, educational psychology and teaching in primary, secondary and special schools. His special interests throughout have been with language development, language disorder and in the last fifteen years, with motor coordination difficulties. He is a contributor for the University of Birmingham distance learning course in speech and language teaching and has recently co-written the NASEN Spotlight book on speech and language difficulties. He also sits on the AFASIC advisory committee and is currently an educational psychologist with Brighton and Hove Council.

Jenny Barrett is qualified both as a speech and language therapist and a teacher. She has worked both in this country and in Canada, and for the last fifteen years, has specialised in specific language disorder. She is a contributor to several research projects, has undertaken postgraduate studies and has written a book for parents, *Help Me Speak – A Parent's Guide to Speech and Language Therapy* (Souvenir Press, Human Horizon Series). She is currently chief speech and language therapist for services to education and preschool special needs in her department at the South Downs Health Trust in East Sussex.

Chapter 1

What is Dyspraxia?

Praxis is a Greek word which is used to describe the *learned* ability *to plan* and *to carry out sequences* of *coordinated movements* in order to achieve an objective.

Dys is the Greek prefix 'bad' so dyspraxia literally means bad praxis.

A child with difficulties in learning skills such as eating with a spoon, speaking clearly, doing up buttons, riding on a bike or handwriting may be described as dyspraxic. The movements which are involved in these activities are all skilled movements which are voluntary and may be affected by dyspraxia. *Voluntary movements*, unlike *reflexes*, are under the conscious control of the individual who carries them out.

Developmental dyspraxia is found in children who have no clear neurological disease. This book is about *movement* problems in children which are complex and involve various poorly understood aspects of how the body and the brain work.

Box 1.1
A formal definition of dyspraxia by a neurologist:

A disorder of the higher cortical processes involved in the planning and execution of learned, volitional, purposeful movements in the presence of normal reflexes, power, tone, co-ordination and sensation (Miller 1986).

Some researchers (Dawdy 1981) describe children with developmental dyspraxia as showing impaired performance of skilled movements despite abilities within the average range and no significant findings on standard neurological examination. Other researchers have identified links with learning, language, visual-perceptual and behavioural problems (Henderson and Sugden 1992). It is important to remember that all children are different and that some difficulties may not become apparent until specific demands

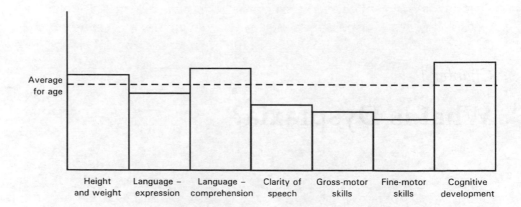

Figure 1.1 A developmental profile

are made, such as learning to use a pencil. A difficulty becomes significant when it interferes with the way that a child is able to carry out the normal range of activities which is expected at his or her age: the usual developmental goals.

The idea of a developmental profile may be helpful when considering a child who has difficulties with coordinated movements (see Fig. 1.1). If motor skills are at a different level from the other areas of development, there may be a specific problem such as developmental dyspraxia.

The term dyspraxia is used differently by professionals within and across occupational therapy, speech and language therapy, psychology and medicine. There is also a range of other labels which may be used to describe developmental dyspraxia but they have no clear definition (see Fig. 1.2).

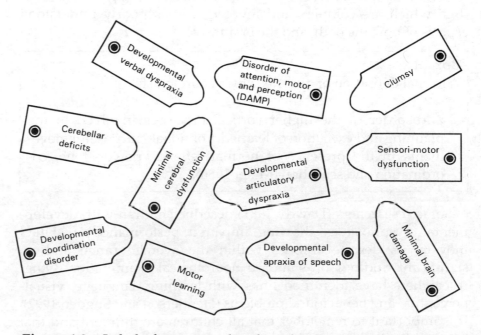

Figure 1.2 Labels that are used to describe developmental dyspraxia

In this book we have used the term *developmental dyspraxia* to refer to difficulties associated with a vital area of development in children, the development of coordination and the organisation of movement. That is, problems with

>   *Getting our bodies to do what we want when we want them to do it.*

Praxis is learned behaviour but it also has a biological component. The sequence of motor development is pre-determined by innate biological factors that occur across all social, cultural, ethnic and racial boundaries (Gallahue 1982). The development of movement abilities is an extensive process which begins with the earliest reflex movements. The developmental schedule for voluntary movements unfolds between the ages of two and twelve years when an adult level of competence is possible. According to Luria, a famous Russian neurologist, the area of the brain which is responsible for simple voluntary movement, e.g. hammering a peg into a hole, is developed on average by four years of age. By six to seven years the area of the brain which is needed for more complex movement combinations is developed. Children with difficulties continue to make more movement errors and *action errors* than other children of the same age.

The sequence of motor development can, however, only become operational by continual interaction with the external environment. The learning of early movement skills usually takes place in the context of play.

How praxis develops

The early learning of movement patterns

Box 1.2
One of the early toys that most babies have is the rattle that parents attach to the pram. A baby will respond to this novelty by showing general excitement which involves random movements of his arms and legs and even the whole body. The movement itself will cause the toy to vibrate and make a noise which in turn stimulates more interest in the toy. An accidental contact with the toy, as a result of the excited movements, will give pleasurable feedback in terms of noise and movement of the toy. In a relatively short time most babies learn how to strike the toy deliberately in order to get it to move and to make a noise. The action of the baby becomes more skilled over time so that one arm, rather than all four limbs, will be involved and it will be used with an increasing degree of control over the force, direction, distance and amplitude of the movement. The baby's movements become better coordinated and more efficient as they become more skilled.

Parents carefully record and even video the motor milestones which their baby achieves but the complexities of the learning of the co-ordinated movements of muscle groups which are required in order to raise the head, to roll over, to sit up, to stand and to walk are lost to most memories. As we watch babies and young children we are aware that a great deal of practice is needed in order to ensure the smooth performance of these skills which come under automatic control for most people at an early age. As older children and adults we don't consciously have to plan how to move our bodies in order to stand up or scratch our nose – we just 'do' it. Learning to drive may be the only time when adults are faced with the complexities of learning a new skill which demands the coordinated action of different parts of the body together with the fine tuning of the force, amplitude and timing of a sequence of movements.

Children with developmental dyspraxia have difficulties acquiring both the early motor skills and learning new, more complex skills. They may, with more practice than others of their age, reach a reasonable level of competence for a specific skill such as placing the pieces in a favourite tray jigsaw, but this skill will not necessarily generalise to other related skills.

Where things might go wrong

Organised physical movement is dependent upon the sensory information which the body receives from its environment. Some sensors operate very early in life, possibly even before birth. The sensors that are important for movement are the:

- tactile receptors;
- vestibular apparatus;
- proprioceptive system.

People are seldom consciously aware of the roles of the vestibular apparatus or the proprioceptive system although information from the tactile receptors may impinge on consciousness as when we tread on a drawing pin. We are more consciously aware of processing the information which we receive from the senses of taste, smell, sound and vision. One theory about dyspraxia (Ayres 1972) gives central

---

Box 1.3 *Tactile receptors*
The tactile receptors are cells in the skin that send information to the brain about light, touch, pain, temperature and pressure.

Box 1.4 *Vestibular apparatus*
The vestibular receptors are found in the inner ear. The vestibular sense responds to body movement in space and changes in head position. It automatically coordinates the movements of eyes, head and body, is important in maintaining muscle control, coordinating the movements of the two sides of the body and maintaining an upright position relative to gravity.

Box 1.5   *Proprioceptive system*
The proprioceptors are present in the muscles and joints of the body and give us an awareness of body position. They enable us to guide arm or leg movements without having to monitor every action visually. Thus, proprioception enables us to do familiar actions such as fastening buttons without looking. When proprioception is working efficiently, adjustments are made continually to maintain posture and balance and to adjust to the environment, for example when walking over uneven ground.

---

importance to the ability to integrate the information which is received from the senses. If this is disrupted the ability to plan and to execute skilled or novel (new) motor tasks may be impaired.

Most researchers (Cermak 1985, Conrad *et al.* 1983) emphasise two elements in developmental dyspraxia:

- ideational or planning dyspraxia;
- ideo-motor or executive dyspraxia.

Dewey and Kaplan (1992) identified three groups of children: Group 1 showed problems in both areas, Group 2 difficulties with the execution of movement patterns and Group 3 difficulties with the planning of sequences of movements.

Conrad *et al.* (1983) divided the individuals with ideational or planning dyspraxia into those who had difficulties with the planning of sequences of movement and those who had difficulties with moving themselves or objects in two- or three-dimensional space. The latter involves *spatial awareness* and *directional awareness* which can present additional problems for some dyspraxic children.

It is probable that all three elements: sensory integration, the planning of action and the execution of the plan, are involved in the

---

Box 1.6

Ideational dyspraxia
This term describes difficulties with the planning of a sequence of coordinated movements or with actions which involve the manipulation of objects. The individual actions may be carried out competently, e.g. hammering the wooden peg, but the order of the actions may be lost, e.g. failing to put the peg in the hole before hammering. In older children organising tasks, equipment and their ideas may become a problem.

Ideo-motor dyspraxia
Children with ideo-motor dyspraxia know what they want to do but find it hard to execute their action plan. The performance of individual actions may be clumsy, slow, awkward, non-fluent and they may experience problems with transition: moving from one action to the next.

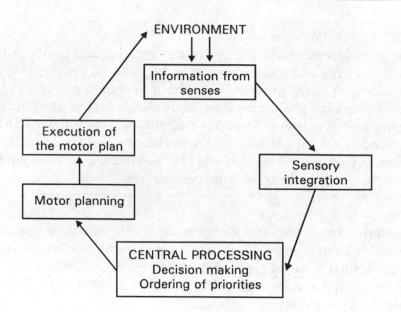

Figure 1.3 The feedback loop for efficient praxis

efficient carrying out of complex sequences of voluntary, coordinated movements. Figure 1.3 shows how all these elements may be inter-related.

For individual children and their carers the picture may be further complicated by the way in which developmental dyspraxia can affect different parts of the motor system. For some children articulatory dyspraxia which affects the intelligibility of their speech may be the main area of difficulty, for others the fine-motor control of their fingers for fastening buttons or for writing and for yet others the co-ordination of the whole body and awareness of its position in space.

This book will show how dyspraxia may affect a child at home: 'My daughter would fall over a blade of grass in a field', and at school where the child is often as puzzled as the teacher about why they can do some things but not others: 'He can write neatly when he tries.'

It will also consider how the daily struggle to control their body as it interacts with the physical and social environment can erode self-esteem and confidence.

Parents say:

- He's so slow I still have to dress him.
- I send him upstairs to get his coat and he starts to play or comes down with the wrong thing.
- I have to buy clothes with velcro fastenings.
- He often puts things on in the wrong order – shoes before trousers.
- He makes such a mess when eating.
- We never arrive on time because I have to hunt for him.
- He is set at one speed – 'slow'.
- He can only do one thing at a time.

Teachers say:
- His books are such a mess.
- He always loses his pencil.
- She can never find her place in the book.
- Why won't he keep his numbers in the right boxes, he can do his sum but only if I write it down.
- He's just the class clown.
- He can't seem to stay on his chair without falling off.
- His shoes are always on the wrong feet, his shirt inside out, back to front and hanging out of his trousers.
- He's never got his kit for PE and is always last into the Hall.
- He puts more paint on him and his friends than on the paper.
- He is more interested in what other people are doing.
- *When he works on the computer, I can begin to see his true ability.*

Children say:
- Someone's nicked my pencil.
- My mum forgot to give me my PE/swimming kit.
- Nobody will play with me.
- I don't like PE.
- It was an accident, Miss, I just bumped into him.
- I left my brain in the taxi today.

Chapter 2

Dyspraxia: a Developmental Perspective

It is important to understand as much as we can about how our brains and bodies function and what might go wrong, but this approach can only provide part of the total picture because we are not standard perfect machines that acquire faults. We are complex and individually unique organisms that develop in a natural and social environment. Increasingly, the picture of ourselves as developing and changing as we grow and age is being seen as the key to human psychology. The core principle of a developmental perspective is that any particular observation about an individual, e.g. this child is poor at copying or drawing crosses and angles, needs instantly to be related to the child's current developmental goals.

> *A developmental goal is the level of performance which the majority of children is expected to be able to achieve at a given age in any area of functioning.*

When we ask questions such as 'why is this child unable to copy crosses or angles?', we may usefully use a fault-finding approach to shape our investigations. This is because a fault-finding approach is not incompatible with the developmental approach, provided that when we think a fault has been identified we refer to the child's developmental goals as the framework within which to consider how best to help. However, when practitioners focus exclusively upon a fault-finding approach, training programmes may be generated that use odd materials and unusual exercises whose purpose may be unclear to the child and this may not be the most efficient way to help skills to generalise into real life. A developmental perspective can guide the planning of support programmes which incorporate the learning opportunities the child needs within the framework of a range of everyday activities.

The development of motor coordination, voluntary movement, consists of an interaction between the gradual unfolding of the brain's pre-set developmental pattern and the learning opportunities

---

Box 2.1 *Key features of a developmental approach*

- Identify the key developmental goal(s) that need to be achieved and if early goals have not been mastered, build up the skills using materials which are appropriate to the age of the child;
- Be aware that children reach developmental goals in different ways and at different ages. Thus, children with good body awareness (proprioceptive sense) may do up buttons early and without looking, whereas a child with poor proprioception may need to look at their hands in order to guide the actions;
- A developmental profile (see p. 2) can summarise how skills such as vocabulary, handwriting, imagination develop separately and at different rates within any individual. Encompassing the developmental profile is the individual's sense of 'self' and anyone working with a child should seek to understand how they see the world, what is important to them and what personal resources they can bring to their own learning. *Central, therefore, to a developmental perspective is self-esteem and personal motivation.*

---

provided by the environment. The brain's own pre-set developmental pattern is fundamental to the way we come to control and direct our movements. The learning opportunities provided by our environment slot into this. This is not well understood in schools and children's difficulties are often mistakenly linked to a lack of practice. Examples may serve to illustrate this.

When children are poor at balance, climbing, ball skills or struggle to take off and put on their clothes, you may hear teachers say one of the following:

- He is always stuck indoors.
- She is never taken to the park.
- His mother babies him – does everything for him.
- He had no preschool experience.
- She was never played with as a baby.
- He doesn't concentrate on what he is doing.

The safest assumption to make is that these statements are never true. The starting point should be that the child's pre-set motor pattern is not developing smoothly, and this should be followed by an assessment of exactly where they are having difficulty. The teachers of poorly coordinated children will often observe their mothers 'doing things for them'. This is because mothers adapt and respond to their own children's needs. Often the teacher can help the mother reflect on the way that they are helping their child and gently introduce more learning into the situation.

Example one: a child appears to be poorly coordinated, clumsy

Example two: handwriting is untidy

The speed and legibility of the handwriting of a seven year old is more dependent on their brain organisation than on any other factor. Despite this, teachers are still more likely to offer one or more of the following explanations:

- He doesn't take care.
- She doesn't concentrate.
- He avoids writing and so never practises.
- She has never been shown how to write.
- He doesn't try.

It is important to remember that children must learn to organise and to control their voluntary movements and that everyone does not progress at the same rate. The brains of some people mature quickly and efficiently in the areas which control movement, but for others this aspect of development may be particularly slow or incomplete. These individual differences are true of all biological variation and perhaps the most obvious one is height. The scientific way of describing the range of individual differences is by means of the 'normal curve' of distribution (see Fig. 2.1).

If we apply the normal curve to motor coordination we find that most people have average coordination, with smaller numbers having very poor or very good coordination. Professional sportspeople invariably have very good all-round coordination regardless of the sports skills they have learned. Some children, therefore, are going to find handwriting easier to learn than others because of their neurology/biology.

The idea of a normal distribution of motor skills may create problems for a view of dyspraxia as a fault in an otherwise standard human model. It may be hard to decide whether a child should be considered to be dyspraxic or just relatively poorly coordinated. At an operational level this may not be a problem as any motor difficulties which are present can be reframed in a developmental and educational perspective by asking and answering the following questions:

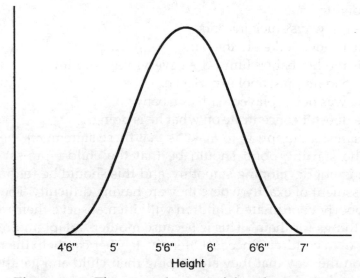

Figure 2.1   The normal curve of distribution: height

- What exactly does s/he have difficulties doing?
- Which processes are, therefore, relatively weak?
- How does this affect his/her functioning and the achievement of developmental goals?
- What strategies can be used to help him/her achieve specified educational and developmental goals?

The most effective way to analyse a child's difficulties is to take into account a fault-finding model and then to consider the information which is obtained from this approach in the context of the developmental perspective. The fault-finding approach can yield important information about types of difficulty which may occur, how they arise and how they are manifested in children. The developmental perspective gives insights into how a particular pattern of functioning can affect the achievement of developmental goals.

For all children the primary goal is to promote self-esteem throughout their development. For children who experience developmental difficulties of any kind it is particularly important to focus upon the establishment of a positive self-image and to maintain self-esteem. The child who is poorly coordinated will usually need more practice to acquire the motor skills which their friends find easy and each child will need different amounts of practice, special teaching and self-esteem protection. Most poorly coordinated children do eventually master skills such as speaking clearly, eating with a knife and fork, riding a bicycle and handwriting. However, careful investigation or changes in environmental demands can reveal that an individual who experienced early problems has skills which are less flexible and more vulnerable under pressure.

Examples

'J, with the help of the speech and language therapist, has developed clear speech but still stumbles over some longer words and is difficult to understand when excited or upset.'

'K did eventually learn to form the letters but his writing is larger than most of his classmates, letter formation is irregular (untidy to the teacher) and he can only write slowly.'

For the two children cited in the examples the developmental goals have been reached and their performance is 'good enough' under everyday conditions. Their performance may be incapable of further improvement or the remaining small gains in performance may not be cost effective in terms of the time and effort needed to produce those gains. In the case of 'K' it may be appropriate to accept current skill levels and adapt to the changing demands of the curriculum by considering alternative means of recording. A very few individuals will not achieve the developmental goals.

During childhood old problems may seem to disappear and new ones arise simply because the developmental goals change. Thus, at six years a child with poor coordination may have difficulties in the playground because play at that age is often quite physical, particularly among boys. At twelve years the same child may appear to have fewer problems at playtime because the focus of free time has changed to become more conversational. However, the early experiences of difficult playtimes may leave a legacy of low self-esteem and diffident, unrewarding relationships with peers.

Low self-esteem can affect how an individual faces new challenges and strives to achieve developmental goals. If the underlying problems and the issues surrounding self-esteem are not addressed, a child at twelve years may have adequate handwriting, no undue playground pressures but have negative feelings about himself/herself as a learner, towards school, towards adults and his/her own future.

Chapter 3

The Assessment of Dyspraxia

The evidence suggests that parents are usually the first to notice their children's difficulties but that it may be hard to have those initial concerns acknowledged by their health visitor, GP or visiting therapists. Some parents will actively seek a label for their child's difficulties whereas others may be alarmed by the idea of a diagnostic label.

The identification of a problem with motor skills

Box 3.1 *Dyspraxia as a diagnostic label*

Advantages	*Disadvantages*
1. Parents may contact support agencies to find out more about their child's difficulties and how to help at home.	1. The child may be seen as dyspraxic rather than as a unique individual with their own pattern of strengths and weaknesses.
2. Information about the condition can be shared with family, friends, teachers.	2. A label such as dyspraxia may restrict the expectations that adults have for the child's development.
3. The problem may be taken more seriously by professionals. *J's slow development was attributed to a lack of stimulation at home by social services until J was identified as dyspraxic.*	3. A label may affect the child's self-perception and self-expectations. Being a special type of person can be a refuge but it can also be a prison.
4. It will help the child's self-esteem to know that s/he is not stupid but does have a recognised problem with which others will help.	

Use the label but don't become trapped by it

Parents are aware of their children as developing individuals and have expectations of what their children should be doing at different ages. Adult friendship groups often centre on having children of a similar age and so comparisons are made between families as a result of normal social interactions. Some parents also have experience about the normal patterns of development from older siblings. If they detect that a child is lagging behind with developmental goals they become concerned and may start by sharing their anxieties with other parents. In Chapter 2 the normal range of development of motor skills was discussed and so for many parents early concerns may resolve themselves in due course. However, a small number of children will show the signs of significant movement difficulties which will need to be identified, assessed and therapeutic intervention planned.

A model for the identification of children with movement difficulties: response to parental concerns

Parent concerns should provide the basis for discussion with a professional who has studied child development. In the UK parents often share their initial concerns with a health visitor. The parent and health visitor, working together, may decide to ask for a referral to a paediatrician and this referral would usually be channelled through the general practitioner. However, not all general practitioners are experts in child development and they rarely carry out the assessment tasks and activities which would show up problems with movement difficulties. Most general practitioners will acknowledge the concerns expressed by the health visitor and proceed with a referral to a neurodevelopmental paediatrician.

Children may be more fortunate if the movement or coordination difficulty shows itself in speech because such children may be referred directly to a speech and language therapist.

Children with difficulties coping with school, self-care and play activities may be referred to an occupational therapist who is specialised in working with children. The occupational therapy services for children are variable across counties, according to resources available from the local health and education authorities.

Clinical and educational psychologists are experts in child development. However, their knowledge and experience rarely tends to focus upon movement and the development of motor coordination.

A model for the identification of children with movement difficulties: response to concerns in school

Once a child starts school the teacher shares the perspective of the parent by being aware of progress towards developmental goals, particularly those which are addressed more at school than at home such as handwriting or play with other children. Since the 1993 Education Act a mechanism for teachers to follow up concerns about a child has been outlined in the Code of Practice for schools. The Code of Practice is grounded in a developmental perspective as it has a focus upon teacher concerns about the progress of a child towards key developmental goals.

The Code of Practice

Stage 1
The teacher shares their concern with the parent and finds out more about the child's developmental history. The teacher adapts their teaching programme in order to help the child reach specific goals, monitors and reviews the child's progress over a period of half a term to a full term.

Stage 2
The teacher remains concerned and now talks to the Special Needs Coordinator (SENCO) and shares the concerns with parents. The SENCO makes suggestions and may arrange some extra help for the child. An Individual Education Plan is drawn up and the targets set out in the plan are monitored and reviewed over a period of half a term to a term. The SENCO has the lead role in coordinating the provision for a child at this stage and has a responsibility to keep the headteacher informed from then on.

Stage 3
If the concern about the child continues, and after consultation with the parents, the child may be referred to an appropriate professional: learning support teacher, educational psychologist, speech and language therapist or school doctor. A new Individual Education Plan is agreed and progress is monitored and reviewed by the SENCO who has the lead role in coordinating the provision which is made for the child.

Stage 4
If the concerns about the child persist over time, the school SENCO, with the consent of the parents, may request a Statement of Special Educational Needs under the 1993 Education Act. Reports are prepared by all the people who have been involved with monitoring the child's progress and the views of the parents are sought. Representatives of the LEA consider the evidence that has been presented and decide whether to proceed with the Statementing process.

The assessment of a problem with motor skills

The Code of Practice provides a framework for the assessment and monitoring over time of the special educational needs of any child. At Stage 3 of the Code of Practice or during the preschool years, a child with developmental dyspraxia may be referred to a range of professionals so that further assessments can be carried out. The purpose of the assessments is to analyse in more detail the difficulties which a child experiences and to plan more effective ways of helping a child and his/her parents and teachers to resolve these difficulties. This may be by developing skills or by finding alternative ways for the child to achieve the appropriate developmental goals.

In Chapter 1 the complexities of developmental dyspraxia were discussed in terms of children who have difficulties with the planning of sequences of movement, those who have difficulties with the execution of movement patterns and those who experience difficulties in both of these areas. The fact that for individual children different areas of their motor system may be more affected than others further complicates the assessments. Thus, a child may be able to do a forward roll in the PE lesson but have great difficulty back in the classroom controlling a pencil.

A child who has been identified as having significant movement difficulties may meet a range of professionals who will tend to focus on different aspects of the child's functioning following the fault-finding model which was discussed in Chapter 2. The results can be a rather fragmented and even contradictory catalogue of evidence that needs to be integrated into a coherent picture of how this child's difficulties affect his/her functioning at home and at school. It is usually the role of the educational psychologist to review the evidence and consider the needs of the whole child in the context of their social, physical and learning environment.

Assessment by the speech and language therapist

Children can be referred for assessment from birth onwards. Speech and language therapists will assess the following areas depending on a child's age. For example, no assessment of speech or language would be needed with a few weeks old baby.

Areas assessed are:
- feeding, eating and drinking;
- oral skills/oral examination;
- speech;
- fluency;
- prosody;
- voice;
- degree of nasality in speech;
- listening and attention skills;
- language;
- other aspects of communication, e.g. non-verbal skills and interactions with others;
- play.

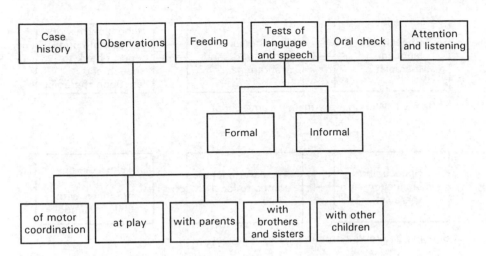

Figure 3.1 Speech and language therapy assessment

The assessment procedure is summarised in Figure 3.1.

If verbal dyspraxia was the suspected diagnosis, certain aspects of communication would be assessed in greater detail. Feeding, the precursor of verbal communication, is discussed in Chapter 4.6.

Others are:

- oral skills;
- the speech sound system;
- sequencing of sounds;
- the control of breathing and phonation (the production of sounds);
- prosodic features of speech (e.g. rate of production, rhythmic quality, pitch, intonation, nasal resonance, volume);
- dribbling.

Speech and language therapists use a wide range of formal and informal tests, profiling procedures and observations as well as taking a comprehensive case history of the child.

Verbal dyspraxia is frequently associated with a more generalised dyspraxia and the therapist would be observing the child's other motor movements. Some children have blank, rather expressionless faces because of difficulties with the coordination of the muscle groups which are needed to signal facial expression (see Chapter 5 for further information). This can have an extremely negative effect on the perception that parents, peers and teachers have of the child as it can be misconstrued from being 'unresponsive' to 'defiant'.

Often speech and language therapists are the first professionals to see a child with dyspraxia because of early feeding difficulties or lack of speech and would refer him/her on for assessment by others if the dyspraxia was affecting other areas of motor development.

There is a range of ways that speech and language therapists may help to support children who experience speech and language difficulties in school and these are summarised in the flow charts (see Fig. 3.2). The level of direct involvement by the speech and language therapist will depend upon the nature and the severity of the child's difficulties.

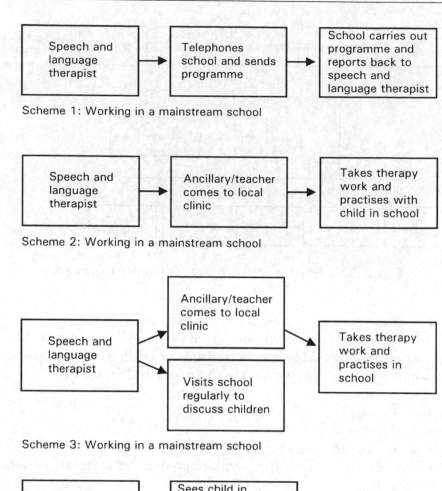

Scheme 1: Working in a mainstream school

Scheme 2: Working in a mainstream school

Scheme 3: Working in a mainstream school

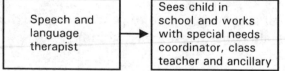

Scheme 4: Working in a mainstream school

Figure 3.2   Delivery of speech and language services to schools

Assessment by the occupational therapist

A child will be referred to an occupational therapist because someone has noticed they have difficulty in coping with school, self-care and/or play activities. For example, handwriting, PE, dressing, using a knife and fork or riding a bicycle. As these children have difficulties in these areas they may also have problems making friends, show poor motivation for some classroom tasks and have low self-esteem.

When assessing a child, the occupational therapist considers their ability to cope in all aspects of life, including home, school and at play. This means that the occupational therapist will discuss the child's abilities with their parents/carer and teacher. This may involve visits to home and observation in school.

A variety of assessments are available to look in more detail at gross- and fine-motor skills, visual perception, handwriting and self-care ability. There are also tests to provide further information about the child's awareness of touch, movement and position of their body in relation to their surroundings. (This involves the proprioceptive, tactile and vestibular senses.)

There are a variety of approaches to intervention that an occupational therapist may use. A very important part of this is the advice and explanations about the child's difficulties which an occupational therapist is able to offer the parent/carer and teacher.

A child can receive treatment either individually or within a group. Programmes may be provided for home and school, and these are individually selected to promote the development of movement skills and the child's independence and self-esteem.

Paediatric assessment

There is a wide range of medical conditions that can give rise to symptoms of dyspraxia. Each child therefore should have a comprehensive medical examination, looking particularly for signs of medical and neurological disease and epilepsy. Neurological examination assesses physical function (muscle tone, reflexes, range of movement, power, involuntary movements, sensations). Developmental assessment is needed to evaluate the child's level of mental functioning against the motor developmental level and to specify particular developmental deficits, for example in language. Checks of vision and hearing are included.

Assessment by the educational psychologist

The educational psychologist will explore how a child is functioning in terms of a developmental perspective. All developmental goals will be considered and not just those which obviously relate to motor functioning such as ball skills or handwriting. This is important because some forms of developmental dyspraxia can affect how children organise their tasks, their equipment and even their ideas, as discussed in Chapter 1. The educational psychologist will use a range of strategies as part of the assessment, which may include:
- a consultation model to collate information which is already available from parents, teachers and other sources;
- observations in a variety of educational and social settings;
- discussion with the child about their self-perception using therapeutic techniques which are appropriate for the age of the child;
- checklists for teachers, parents or self-report which focus upon specific aspects of behaviour or learning;
- individual assessment in order to investigate specific areas of functioning in detail.

Box 3.2   *Individual assessments which may be undertaken by the educational psychologist*

- assessment of cognitive abilities in order to establish areas of strength as well as areas of difficulty and to explore the ways in which a child learns most effectively. A wide range of tasks and tests is available and the psychologist will select those which are most appropriate;
- investigation of aspects of motor functioning and how problems in this area affect the response to the curriculum and relationships with peers. The Movement Assessment Battery for Children (Henderson and Sugden 1992) assesses three main areas of motor skill and, therefore, provides an overview of motor skills: manual dexterity; static and dynamic balance; ball skills.

    Other assessments, such as the test of Visual Motor Integration (Beery 1989) which follows a developmental perspective in measuring the acquisition of pencil skills, have a more specific focus;
- assessment of visual perceptual skills. These are included in generic tests of cognitive ability but some supplementary tests may also be given;
- assessment of educational attainments in core areas of the curriculum such as reading, spelling, handwriting, number skills;
- some analysis of the ability to imitate movement patterns and gestures may be obtained from observation schedules which target PE-type activities and more specific tests.

As evidence for a formal assessment of educational needs and in some cases at Stage 3 of the Code of Practice, the educational psychologist produces a report which sets out in detail the special educational needs of the child together with the facilities and resources which are required in order to meet those educational needs.

A framework for reporting on a child with developmental dyspraxia

- a developmental history which includes motor milestones and information about the acquisition of self-help skills;
- details of any specific therapeutic input from: physiotherapy, occupational therapy, speech and language therapy, child and family services;
- patterns of social interaction, communication and behaviour at home and at school (or playgroup);
- an educational history including responses to preschool experiences and school-based interventions;
- response to the present learning environment in terms of access

to the National Curriculum, educational attainments, social/emotional response to learning, motivation;

- analysis of cognitive abilities and preferred learning style;
- views of the child and parents to include exploration of the child's self-esteem, interests and areas of success;
- special educational needs in the context of overall levels of functioning;
- the facilities and resources required to meet the special educational needs.

Chesson *et al.* (1991) found that the educational psychologist had a key role in the identification of dyspraxia in children but that the children in their study had seldom been referred to the educational psychologist before they started school. They also found that more referrals to the occupational therapists were initiated by the educational psychologists than by any other professional group.

Observational guidelines to help with the identification of children with motor organisational problems are presented in the appendix.

Chapter 4

The Development of Voluntary Movement and How to Help

Introduction

In this section the development of voluntary movement will be considered together with strategies for helping those children who experience delay and difficulty in acquiring the skills involved.

A baby arrives in the world with very little control over its own body. The infant gradually gains control over its body in the presence of gravity and learns to stabilise the body and move with control.

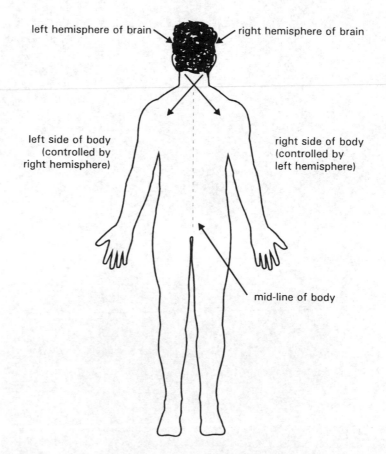

left hemisphere of brain

right hemisphere of brain

left side of body
(controlled by
right hemisphere)

right side of body
(controlled by
left hemisphere)

mid-line of body

Figure 4.1 The relationship between brain and body

As a toddler a new aspect of control begins to develop. The left and right sides of the body are controlled from the two different halves of the brain; left side – right brain and right side – left brain. Our body, therefore, has an imaginary line running down it which is called the mid-line (see Fig. 4.1). The organisation of our movements around this mid-line is vital to the learning of skilled physical actions. From around eighteen months to six years we are developing this aspect of control. Much of this centres on stabilising the trunk and working out what each arm and hand is going to do while performing such complex tasks as eating with a spoon, opening doors, doing up buttons, pouring and writing. These complex tasks are more accurately and reliably carried out if one hand becomes skilled and practised at fiddly tasks while the other hand helps by holding things steady, taking the weight, etc. This we recognise as developing a hand preference. For most individuals the right hand becomes skilled, with the left hand taking the support role.

At six years, for most children, basic motor organisation is complete and the child can concentrate on using the control over their body and its movements that they have already achieved in order to learn specific skills such as writing, dancing and sports skills such as football and tennis. The last complex skill to be acquired is usually driving.

The most complex skills that we all acquire are speaking and writing. Speaking involves the rapid organisation of numerous muscles. It takes a long time and a lot of practice to master.

Not surprisingly, children who have difficulties in establishing control over their bodies are very likely to show this in their speech. Dyspraxia is, therefore, often first identified and described by speech and language therapists. In writing, the arm, wrist and finger muscles have to learn to make numerous small rapid movements. The development of skilled writing begins with scribbling, holding a crayon in the fist, and continues until the basic skills are acquired by six or seven. Even then the speed at which we can write goes on getting faster, and hence more skilled, until our late teens. Children with handwriting difficulties are sometimes identified as dyspraxic by doctors and occupational therapists.

Complex patterns of movement also occur in a whole range of other situations but we are less conscious of them because most of the coordination required appears to be involuntary, i.e. it happens without us being aware of it:

- when we move our eyes to look at things, i.e. the eyes have to move together;
- when we balance on our feet – there are many muscles in our whole body which are involved;
- when we express our feelings – there are many muscles in our face.

The development of a skill is about practice and the major aim of practice is to reduce the extent to which we have to think about what we are doing. We want our movements to become automatic.

Through practice many of our skilled movements become like involuntary actions such as moving both eyes at the same time. We may carry them out without thinking but some children who have difficulties with the voluntary control of their movements do not quickly bring these apparently involuntary movements under automatic control.

In this chapter the development of voluntary movement has been divided into a number of areas that relate to important aspects of children's lives:

1. Whole body movement, coordination and body image
2. Physical play
3. Dressing
4. Handwriting and drawing
5. Speech and language
6. Feeding and eating

Each of these areas is reviewed using three perspectives: overview; stages of development and helping strategies. Before proceeding, however, some observations are needed.

The stages of development show some of the major landmarks in the child's mastery of an area. For children who experience difficulty the stages can be used to establish the point they have reached and the next stage to target. It is often better to aim at the next stage rather than at the final goal. Teachers will recognise this approach as step-by-step teaching. Alongside the landmarks are written the years and months at which 'on average' children can achieve them. These should be taken as only crude indicators as in reality, children progress at different rates.

The helping strategies always divide into two groups:

- strategies that help the child master the skill;
- strategies that allow the child to compensate for their difficulty in some way.

It is always worth thinking in terms of these two aspects even when a strategy might work for both. For example, a rubber triangle on a pencil might allow the child to write, when without it they would struggle. At the same time, because they can write more easily, they have a chance to practise the movements needed to form letters. Many strategies do, however, only work for one aspect. For example, fitting stabilisers to a bicycle allows the child to ride on it but it does nothing to help the child to master the skill of riding a bicycle. Similarly, putting clothes pegs on the edge of a tin may help the child strengthen their fingers and hence contribute to learning to write but it does nothing to help the child achieve a task that requires writing. A clothes peg is not a pencil.

The strongest focus has been given to the strategies which relate to the major developmental goals of speaking and handwriting. It is in these two areas of development that children with dyspraxia experience the most difficulty and the greatest pressure to perform.

This section is concerned with the child's development of control over their large muscles and hence the coordination of arms, legs, head and trunk. However, groups of small muscles are also involved, for example, in helping to keep balance in the feet or the hand grasping which is involved in large movements such as climbing.

The major developmental targets are walking, running, climbing and jumping. These first develop as isolated skills and are then pushed to their limits in play/practice:

- running while weaving in and out of obstacles and people;
- combining swift changes of movement direction with keeping balance.

A significant small group of children will not yet be skilful at running, climbing and jumping when they enter school. The majority of children will have yet to master hopping and skipping. However, it is the presence of other moving children in the playground that calls for the greatest skill in whole body movement and the clumsy child can quickly stand out from their peers. Similarly, in games and PE lessons, poor skill can look to the teacher like deliberate fooling about and disruption. For some children the development of skilled movement is beyond them and they begin to lose out in the acquisition of sports skills at an early stage. The other children are usually very aware of skill differences. When children are asked to pick teams, it is apparent how acutely aware they are of who has good control over their voluntary movements and who hasn't. As children get older they can choose to avoid social activities that involve skilled physical movement and sports skills but they are still exposed in PE and games lessons. Early experiences of failure can result in a child having little confidence in the ability of their body to learn new skills. There is a strong case for giving special help to this group of children. Experience with motor-skill groups has shown that when these children are taught for some of the time together they feel comfortable and can aim for personal goals. Also, with a careful choice of apparatus and additional support they can develop greater voluntary control, reach objectives on apparatus or in a defined skill area and renew their confidence in their own body. Large self-esteem changes have been noted in children supported in this way. Interested teachers, physiotherapists and occupational therapists are increasingly running groups and clubs for poorly coordinated children and private clubs and groups are also more commonly available.

Special coordination groups for children of secondary age are a different matter. Through a combination of avoidance, pursuit of alternative interests and playground practices, adolescents can avoid being confronted by their motor limitations. They attempt to build their self-esteem elsewhere. Some adolescents continue for a while in out-of-school groups while others invest a great deal of effort into one sports skill at which they eventually reach a socially acceptable level of proficiency – swimming, table tennis, pool, etc. The only time a group or individual programme should be provided for a secondary age

Section 1: Whole body movement, coordination and body image

child is if they ask for it. An exception to this rule is for handwriting which is dealt with in a separate section.

The basic approach to helping children of school age with poor whole body movement is to concentrate on specific areas of skill. Sports skills are acquired as a result of building up complex and fluent patterns of movement. In the same way, learning to roller skate, skip or ride a bicycle can be treated as important personal objectives that a poorly coordinated child can reach if they have the task broken down and are offered supported practice. Children with poor motor development have brain systems that make it hard to learn and to carry out good voluntary control of their movements. This can be seen in a range of ways:

- not remembering the next movement in a sequence;
- not combining movements well;
- poor timing and balance.

Often children with poor motor control find it hard to maintain stillness in their body. Similarly they cannot focus sharply on one area of their body and control spreads to other areas:

- when writing with their hand their tongue moves;
- the support arm and hand twitch and move slightly as the dominant hand makes voluntary movements.

These are called associated movements and the way in which the brain messages generalise to other areas of the body makes it very difficult for the children to learn rapid accurate patterns of movement.

Box 4.1 *Coordination skill groups*

The most important points about motor coordination groups are as follows:

- all selected children should lack confidence in voluntary movement control;
- the activities should vary so as to require different basic skills, i.e. balance, climbing, crawling, sliding, rolling, hand coordination, finger skills and ball control;
- activities can be set up using a wide range of apparatus. Be flexible and creative in their use. Help the children set personal targets. Keep a limited range of activities with small variation every session so that children can work towards their targets. Their skills become focused on the activity you set up and the equipment that you provide;
- provide physical support while children attempt activities. The best principle is to help the child reach the goal initially with a lot of support and then gradually reduce and remove the support as the child's skill develops;
- whole body movement activities benefit from the use of standard school gym equipment. Be careful of the safety issues of using equipment not designed for climbing, jumping, etc.

It is usually helpful to fix on particular objectives and help the child reach these. They may remain poorly coordinated but they can now walk on a balance beam unaided or ride their bicycle. Motor coordination clubs are a good place to set and practise to achieve these personal movement goals. The general approach of teaching to specific personal movement goals is more appropriate than generally attempting to improve the child's motor coordination. The latter approach is an unrealistic and unfocused target given the nature of the children's difficulties.

Body image has two aspects. Firstly, the ability to control specific parts of the body. As we have established earlier in this chapter, the

---

Box 4.2 *Useful equipment for coordination skill groups*

- plastic hoops – jump/hop in various directions, various distances;
- hedgehog ball (with soft plastic spikes) – makes catching much easier;
- pick-up-sticks – these support fine-motor control and individual finger work;
- clothes pegs on a can/peg trains – finger work and hand/hand–eye coordination;
- bean bags – for a variety of 'balance' challenges, such as on head or one foot;
- mats – for rolling under control in different directions;
- benches – for balance, either way up will increase/decrease skill level;
- balloons – these travel more slowly and allow more reaction time for tennis;
- simple step – for gentle toning of leg muscles;
- coins – manipulation and manual dexterity – the coin is the reward for success?
- matchsticks – as with coins and pick-up-sticks;
- peg board – manipulation/shape, pattern, colour matching;
- various sizes of beads threaded on everything from the wire from coat hangers to string;
- canes – stepping over, like hoops (crawling under if cane supported on tripods – spatial awareness);
- basket for throwing balls in – alter the distance as success develops;
- blindfolds – trust games;
- balls of various sizes – for catching but also for rolling and chasing;
- crosses – objects can be put top right, bottom left, can move clockwise or anti-clockwise;
- pairs challenges – simple 'shape' tasks where one partner has to tell the other where the pieces go – no hands;
- tiddlywinks – fine control;
- jump rope – coordination – various heights and speeds.

> **Box 4.3** *Suitable games for co-ordination skill groups*
> - Simon Says;
> - tag;
> - I went shopping and I bought . . .
> - pass the bean bag, 1 bag, 2 bags, etc. in a circle trying to catch up;
> - parachutes;
> - trains – pushing and pulling, back to back;
> - birthday presents – 'unwrap' a body.

child begins with the top and centre of their body and extends control downwards and outwards. For poorly coordinated children the controlled separation of body parts is hard to achieve and while moving one limb sympathetic movements may occur in others. The final areas of individual control are the middle and small fingers. Many adults cannot easily separately control these and they tend to move together.

The second aspect of body image is the naming of the parts so that the child and other people can use language to control movement, e.g. touch your nose with your right hand. As this example shows, as well as labelling body parts the child has to label the two sides of their body as left and right. Other important naming is concerned with turning a quarter, a half, three-quarters, the whole way round. There is a wide range of vocabulary used to describe movement possibilities, i.e. bend, stand on, circle, spread, wiggle, shake and touch. Verbal instructions given to children and the learning of names should follow the development of control. Although in the normal pattern of development naming comes after control, for older children who experience difficulties, naming and verbal instruction can be used to help the development of control, for example in games such as Simon Says. Verbal naming should approximate to a developmental order.

When talking to children with poor coordination and giving them

> **Box 4.4** *Order of naming: body parts and movement*
> *Preschool* – body, head, legs, arms, hand, foot, bend, roll, sit, crawl, stand, walk, run, throw, jump.
> *Early school* – wrist, finger, palm, elbow, knee, shoulder, ankle, toes, stretch, trace, circle, turn, twist, reach, left, right, hop, skip, crouch, stoop.

directions or instructions, their control levels need to be taken into account. Ideally they are learning the words and the verbal instructions that will help them to develop control over their bodies.

Timing is a vital aspect of skilled movement. It is extremely difficult to separate from rhythm, so inevitably music can help children to time their movements through its rhythmic aspects. This is, of course, the nature of dance and dancing is, therefore, very helpful in developing movement control. It is rarely used for poorly coordinated children but it has great potential for this purpose.

Though we have considered whole body movement in the context of air we also need to be aware of the possibilities of coordinated voluntary movements in water. In air the basis of controlled movement is balance, in water it is floating. Little motor control is required to achieve successful floating. Confidence and getting the feel of being in water is fundamental and even babies can achieve this. At any age learning to float is the starting point. After this, movement through and in water is a matter of mastering the control of physical movements as on land. The easiest standard swimming stroke to master is the back stroke but many children do not have the confidence to start with this stroke as they prefer to be on their fronts. The hardest is the breast stroke. Some children's confidence in their body almost solely resides in their ability to swim and it is an area of potential mastery for even the most poorly coordinated child. Children can maintain their self-esteem with only one or two clear areas of mastery and success. Swimming is a key area in which children with poor coordination can set and achieve personal goals of body control. The relatively slow movements made in water gives time to organise movement patterns and breathing. It is also a social sport whereby, providing water confidence is acquired, poorly coordinated children can participate in swimming and fun activities in an almost identical way to more coordinated children. It is one sport which does not have to be competitive.

Another important aspect of whole body movement concerns the issue of physical fitness and exercise. Through avoiding the opportunities to develop voluntary movement older children can opt out of fitness and physical health. Young children do maintain physical health and a degree of fitness through play, running, climbing and jumping and as the children get older these are gradually replaced by sports skills. Unfortunately, most of these are competitive. It is vital that all children find areas of confident voluntary movement control in order to exercise.

Whole body movement and coordination

Developmental milestones
5 mths	transfers object from hand to hand;
6 mths	can roll over;
8 mths	when held upright, steps by putting one foot in front of the other;
1 yr	pulls self to stand, walks around furniture stepping sideways; crawls on hands and knees;
13 mths	climbs on a ledge or low step;
15 mths	walks alone;
1 yr 6 mths	runs stiffly upright, eyes fixed on the ground, cannot continue round obstacles; creeps backwards down stairs;

	beginning to jump, both feet;
	throws without falling;
2 yrs	picks up an object without falling;
2 yrs 6 mths	jumps from a bottom step with both feet together;
3 yrs	can run round obstacles and corners even when pushing a large toy;
3 yrs 6 mths	can walk on tiptoe;
	walks downstairs one step at a time;
4 yrs	walks downstairs one foot per step;
	skips and hops on one foot;
4 yrs 6 mths	can jump over a small obstacle;
5 yrs	can skip and hop two or three yards on either foot;
	active and skilful in climbing, swinging, jumping, sliding, digging and 'stunts';
6 yrs	can use skates;
	can jump landing on toes only;
	can walk and jump backwards;
	jumps over a low rope;
	can skip and hop;
	can use a bat to hit a ball;
	walks balance beam unaided.

Developmental sequence

Whole body movement develops in the following sequence:

rolling ➡ sitting ➡ crawling ➡
kneeling ➡ standing ➡ walking ➡
running ➡ throwing ➡ jumping ➡
hopping ➡ skipping.

Section 2: Physical play

The nature of physical play is directly related to the child's level of motor control and as children reach new possibilities in what they can do they find endless opportunities to practise. It is this practice that adults describe as play. Clearly much of this in the area of voluntary movement is concerned with opportunities to walk, run, climb, jump, etc. In this section we have concentrated on the types of physical play that use objects. The major areas are:

- the development of ball skills. These lead into the school and adult fields of sport;
- the mastery of wheels: tricycles, bicycles, roller skates, skateboards, etc. Some sports skills link to these also;
- the development of manipulative skills such as pouring, the use of scissors, threading and sewing, making connections (such as in constructional material and some toys), drawing (a section on its own) and the use of a wide range of tools, hammers, saws, pincers, brushes, etc.

Ball skills form a major area of children's play and activity and by following simple guidelines adults can help to develop these skills:

- the size of the ball being used must correspond to the child's skill level;
- special balls can be bought that are covered in soft rubber spikes which makes them much easier to catch;
- the closer the adult stands to the child the easier it is to catch and receive. The adult has to throw the ball straight to the hands for a small child to catch successfully. If the adult moves away the ball comes less accurately and faster. The child then has to move the whole body position in order for the hands to be in the right place to catch the ball and so the catching position is lost. This is because maintaining a good catching position with one's hands requires initially a stable body;
- mistiming is very apparent when observing children who are learning to catch. Standing very near allows the child to close their hands as they see the ball leave the adult's hands. If the adult is too far away they have to sight the moving ball to catch successfully and this is a much higher level of skill.

In reception classes a wide range of ball skills can be observed although usually all the children are given the same activity. Particularly in the early years, children's *self-esteem relies more on success than on doing the same activity as everyone else*. A clear programme for the development of ball skills is required which allows the children to progress from activity to activity and from level to level and experience success for themselves and in the eyes of their classmates. Interestingly, football training shows how this can be done for foot control using special activities and tasks.

Though ball skills continue into school the mastery of wheels does not. This is seen as an area of play and although some play equipment in schools is wheeled no teaching is involved. Children practise play endlessly on wheels. The right size of tricycle or bicycle is the critical feature here; the child's toes should just touch the ground on both sides.

The development of manipulative skills such as pouring takes place through sand and water play. Constructional material usually requires good spatial ability as well as good fine-motor control. Spatial ability can most easily be understood as seeing what to do. Each tool has its own combination of spatial judgement, movement control and clear separate roles for both hands. The use of each tool requires practice. Scissors should be viewed as a complex tool that takes a great deal of practice to master. There is often a conflict between child safety and the development of skilled scissor use. An adult would often find it hard to cut with children's scissors and any pair that will not cut should be rejected. Remember that left handers require left-handed scissors and that paper thickness relates directly to finger strength and hence to cutting difficulty. The need to pull with the thumb and push with the fingers while cutting in order to keep the blades tight and the need to hold the paper (or anything else which is to be cut) in the correct place should be explained, demonstrated and supported practice given if this is required.

Box 4.5 *Scissor skills*
1. A variety of scissors is available:
   easy grip;
   self-opening;
   left-handed;
   teaching scissors – right and left handed;
   double-handed scissors so that teacher and child can cut together.
   Available from Taskmaster Ltd, Morris Road, Leicester LE2 6BR.
2. Grade the paper:
   stiff paper – 80gsm/90gsm is the easiest to cut
   work towards less stiff paper . . . material
   　　　　　　　　stiffer paper . . . cardboard.
3. If s/he finds it hard to cut along a line, stick card on to the back of the paper to act as a scissor guide.
4. Grade the tasks:
   (a) simple snips at the edge of a card – make a fringe
   　　　　　　　　　　　　　　make a centipede;
   (b) two black lines half an inch apart – cut between them, make a spiral/snail;
   (c) reduce the distance between the lines;
   (d) follow the line;
   (e) combine lines and simple curves;
   (f) demonstrate how to make left and right turns (cut–stop–change direction–cut);
   (g) combine line/curve/turn;
   (h) cut out simple shapes;
   (i) cut round the edge of a picture;
   (j) cut out shapes within a picture;
   (k) make scrapbooks, collages, etc., using a variety of materials;
   (l) model making – craft, design and technology projects.

(Dunn 1979)

Physical play

Developmental milestones

6 mths	shakes objects deliberately to make sounds;
1 yr	places one object on another;
	uses both hands freely;
1 yr 6 mths	beginning to show a preference for one hand;
	throws a ball without falling over followed by kicking a ball without falling over;
2 yrs	can pour water from one cup into another;

2 yrs 6 mths	pulls and pushes large toy skilfully but has difficulty steering round obstacles;
3 yrs	can pedal a tricycle;
	cuts with scissors;
4 yrs	throws a ball overhand;
	runs to kick a ball;
	expert rider of a tricycle;
6 yrs	bounces a ball in one hand and catches in two hands;
6 yrs 6 mths	can ride a bicycle.

As the child develops control over their body so their dressing skills develop. At each stage we need to judge the child's level of skill and help them push a little further. When children participate in their own dressing it takes longer. Children's practice can be cut short by busy adults who are clock watching. Sometimes this cannot be avoided. Nevertheless, occasions should be found when the child can go at their own pace.

Motor-delayed children often begin school with incomplete dressing skills. While continuing to work on these at home, the child should be sent to school with clothes that they can largely manage. This calls for velcro fastenings for shoes, stretch tops that don't need buttons, jumpers rather than cardigans and elasticated waistbands or zip flies on trousers. Children's self-esteem and self-image can be adversely affected if they are the one who is still struggling with their clothes when their classmates have moved on to the next activity. At school independence in dressing and undressing is more important than the level of skill that the clothes require.

The last skills to master are tying shoelaces and ties. These can be reached as late as eleven or twelve for some children. This is well outside the normal range and children will be very self-conscious about their failure to reach these developmental goals.

Section 3: Dressing

Dressing and body image

Developmental milestones

1 yr	child sits or sometimes stands without support while dressing;
1 yr 6 mths	pulls off socks, unfastened shoes, etc.;
2 yrs	helps actively with all dressing movements;
2 yrs 6 mths	removes unfastened coat;
	puts on simple clothing such as vest and pants;
3 yrs	unbuttons buttons that are easy to get to;
	puts on shoes and coat without help;
3 yrs 6 mths	buttons up clothes;
4 yrs	dresses and undresses except for back buttons and laces;
5 yrs 6 mths	can tie shoelaces.

Activities to support dressing skills

- backward chaining: teach the last action first and work backwards. For example,
  stage one: put the sock on the child's foot
  child pulls up the sock;
  stage two: put the sock on the foot as far as the instep
  child pulls sock over the foot, etc.
  'You do the last little bit.'
- easy fastenings;
- clothes not too tight;
- clothes placed on the bed, as if on the body;
- clothes placed left to right in the order to put them on;
- clothes placed inside a hoop when undressing for PE;
- no fiddly fastenings – belts, laces, bows.

The occupational therapist may provide additional advice on specific difficulties that individual children may have with dressing.

Section 4: Handwriting and drawing

Handwriting is a fundamental motor skill for children to acquire and it is an example of maturationally controlled behaviour. This means that the motor skills which underpin writing follow a regular sequence of development which emerges as the child matures neurologically. Some learning is, of course, required but the learning cannot be significantly speeded up by coaching. The motor skills required for handwriting are, therefore, more linked to the neurological development of a child than to factors such as motivation, attitude or concentration. A negative attitude towards writing tasks may reflect underlying problems with the mechanics of handwriting which make the activity difficult and unrewarding for the child. The more difficult the mechanics of handwriting are for the individual, the more practice will be needed in order to master the skill but there is no direct relationship between how well most children write and how much practice they have had with writing.

The orderly progression of skill development is illustrated by the designs below:

Group one

Group two

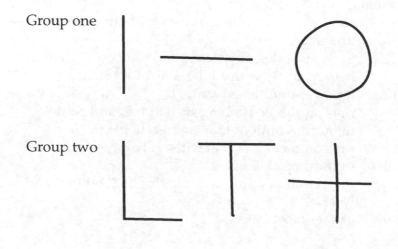

Group three

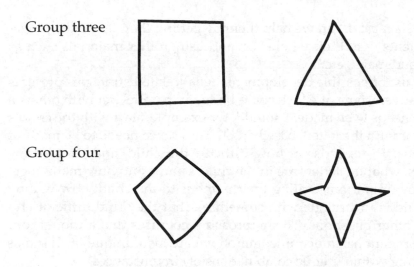

Group four

Children cannot copy or draw a later group until they have learnt the earlier groups. So any child who can draw group four will be able to draw all the designs in one, two and three. A child who cannot draw the designs in group one cannot draw any of the designs in two, three and four.

Groups one and two need to be mastered before letters are attempted and the order of difficulty of letters can be determined by consideration of the sequence. There should be more awareness of this in the teaching of handwriting.

If a five year old is not yet copying crosses and angles we know that they are going to find it more difficult than most children to master the writing of letters and numbers. Any or all of the following conclusions can be drawn:

- The child may well take longer to learn how to write them. They will compare themselves unfavourably with their peers.
  Action point: how can we protect their self-esteem and encourage them to keep trying and not give up?
- The child may need to be given the learning task in small doses. There are fewer numbers to learn than letters and once mastered the child can do quite a lot of independent number work.
  Action point: let's teach them numbers first.
- Some letters are more easily made than others.
  Action point: let's teach them these first, i.e. those based on a circle – o, c, a.
- Letters can be divided into families depending on how they are made. Above are the ones based on circles; others, for example, are based on a 'wiggly' pattern – m, n, w.
  Action point: let's teach the writing of the letters in these families.
- The most important early goal for a child is learning how to write their name.
  Action point: regardless of how difficult the letters are to make, let's give them lots of practice in the letters they need to write their name.
- Analyse the movement patterns the child has to make in order to write the letters.

Action point: can we help them by getting them to do the movements with their whole arm and using other materials such as sand, paint, etc.?

The list of possible developmental goal related strategies presents alternatives, some of which could be run in parallel but with others a choice needs to be made. Should I, for example, start with the child's name or with the letters based on O? The choice needs to be made at the time. It depends on how difficult the child finds it to draw crosses, what the letters are in the child's name and how many there are, how important writing their name is to the child, how willing the child is to struggle with something that they find difficult and many other questions. This approach recognises that although our development has much in common we are also unique individuals operating within unique combinations of circumstances.

Handwriting is a fundamental educational goal basic to progress through the school system. All ages of children spend over a third of their time at school handwriting (Alexander 1992). Five and six year olds spend thousands of hours practising to gain mastery over these complex motor patterns. A few individuals continue into the late primary and secondary phases of education with very poor handwriting skills. The curriculum demands involve an increase in the speed of writing which is required particularly at the point of secondary transfer and most children will write faster and faster until they leave formal education. Pupils' limitations in writing are underidentified in schools and teachers do not always realise how fast children need to write in lessons. They fail to get full notes, don't get down their homework, fail to cover all the points when making a written response in class and struggle to write enough in essays.

In this section we are considering the development of handwriting as a skill. Three broad phases can be identified: the early phase, the middle phase and the final phase.

Early phase

- Establishing a dominant hand and a support hand.
- Mastering the thumb and two finger grip.
- Learning the basic movement patterns for the letters and numbers.

Establishing a dominant hand and a support hand
By five years, children should have hand dominance. The orientation of symbols (letters and numbers) on a page is difficult to do without a dominant side; for example, the horizontal line in a number seven starts on the left and travels to the right, while in a number five it proceeds from the right to the left. Children with no difficulties but without clear dominance can reverse numbers, figures, words and whole sentences. Hand dominance is necessary to enable one hand to practise in a specialist way the complex patterns. There is also a role

for the support hand to learn in moving and holding the paper in position. Children at five years should be encouraged to use just one hand for writing. Left-handed children should experience no special difficulties providing they are given elbow room on tables and desks and provided that they adopt the correct paper position. The 'hook' left-hand grip is a simple result of the right-handed paper position being adopted. When writing, all the letters of the word being written need to be seen. Right handers can see what they are writing because the pen moves away from them. If a left hander uses the right-handed paper position the pen moves towards and across them. A left-handed writer should have the paper to the left and angled at 45 degrees to the vertical.

The best way to correct a left-handed grip that covers what is being written is to move the paper round gradually while holding the pencil further up the stem. Without guidance, by ten or eleven left handers have developed their own strategies, often the hook.

Mastering the thumb and two finger grip

Children begin using drawing and writing tools in their palms. It is usually adults who introduce them to the tripod grip. Initially, despite using a three finger grip, children will make the letter patterns by moving their hand and arm more than their fingers. Skilled writing involves finger and wrist movements with only a sliding action of the arm. In the early phase the grip is the important goal. A minority of children find the grip too difficult as it allows the pencil to wander freely unless good motor control is used. These children often adopt a grip that consists of placing the thumb and both fingers on the stem of the pencil. This variation is not as flexible but it serves the purpose. Poor hand coordination can lead to other unusual grips, for example, with the pencil set between the first and second fingers. After a period of helping the child adopt the correct position the

---

Box 4.6 *Writing left handed*
Rules round-up: ten-point plan
1. Select a writing surface and chair, suitable for your own height.
2. Sit towards the right of the desk or table, leaving plenty of space for writing on the left side of your midline.
3. Place the writing paper to the left of your body midline.
4. Tilt the paper up to 32 degrees in a clockwise direction.
5. Select a writing tool which moves smoothly across the paper.
6. Do not select a pen with a metallic and/or slippery barrel.
7. Support the paper with the right hand.
8. Position the writing tool in a 'below the line' position.
9. Keep the writing forearm parallel with the paper edge as you write.
10. Hold the writing tool sufficiently far from the point to ensure that you can see what you are writing.

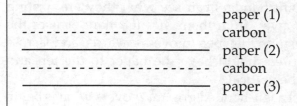
child's preference should be followed. Indeed one of the leading experts on handwriting, Rosemary Sassoon (Sassoon and Briem 1993), argues that the pen held between the first and second fingers may well be a more appropriate position for modern pens. She counsels against rigid adherence to the tripod grip. This alternative grip was used more widely in the past, particularly in classical times. It is a firmer grip but less flexible.

Developing the grip is facilitated by teachers of young children in a number of ways:

- thicker than average pencils;
- triangular shaped thick pencils;
- soft plastic triangular pencil grips that slip on to standard pencil;
- moulded hard plastic grips that have indented thumb and finger positions, for standard pencils.

A triangular rather than a rounded stem encourages the correct grip. Children with poor control who have a tight grip with heavy pressure on the pencil usually benefit from the soft triangular grips while those with difficulties in learning the finger skills required benefit most from the moulded grips. Generally children should be allowed to experiment especially as six and seven year olds while assistance in helping the grip is continuing. Beyond seven years options are severely reduced. Sometimes elastic bands placed round a pen to thicken it can prove beneficial. A lump of Blu-tack is often more acceptable to older pupils and easy grip and self-grip pens have recently become available in the form of both biros and roller balls.

Learning basic movement patterns for letters and numbers
Learning the movement patterns is at the heart of the task. They are learnt initially in the whole arm and transferred down to the hand where in skilled writing they are exclusively located. The course

of this process can be observed in the changes in size of children's writing. Initial large writing is due to arm movements predominating while standard writing is produced by wrist and finger movements only. For most children their writing will gradually become smaller as control over the movement is transferred in stages to the fingers. This process is normally completed by seven or eight years. Sometimes children make a sudden switch from large writing to small writing. This is always a sudden switch from arm to hand control. It is usually found in poorly coordinated children who have found it hard to learn the movement patterns and occurs around seven. The best way to help children become skilled handwriters is to work on the movement patterns through whole arm movements while at the same time building the strength and flexibility of the hand and fingers through appropriate exercises and games. Clearly a third element remains straightforward practice at handwriting. We have listed strategies for helping the child's arm learn the movement patterns and strategies for hand and finger skills at the end of this section.

Teaching handwriting

- *The traditional British way:* At the infant phase, handwriting is the copying of individual letters, printing. At about seven a cursive script is taught whereby movement patterns that link the letters are added and complete movement patterns learned for words. Adult writers tend to retain some letter separations so that a full cursive hand is rare.
- *The alternative way:* In parts of the world such as continental Europe where children start school later, they learn a cursive script from the start.

Young children in Europe tend to print, which suggests that it is a separate phase of development when it is easier to separate each movement pattern to form individual letters. Movement patterns for whole words and to support spelling are better learned through a cursive script. In addition, handwriting is a flowing movement which is more efficiently executed as a continuous pattern. Handwriting experts generally recommend the teaching of cursive handwriting from the beginning but for children with poor movement control and for young children this may be a difficult target for them to achieve.

Middle phase

The middle phase of handwriting development begins within the first phase and partly parallels it.

- Transferring movement patterns fully into the hand.
- Learning to maintain an even size and to orientate the letters/ words on a line, either real or imaginary.
- Introducing a range of tools.

Transferring movement patterns

We have already discussed some aspects of the transfer of movement patterns into the hand. This can be encouraged by providing lined paper when children reach the age of six years. The introduction of lined paper has to be carried out carefully. At first children need to write on plain paper so that they can produce the letters according to the size dictated by their arm and hand movements. The process of transferring handwriting skill into the hand varies between children hence the size of their writing varies. Lines impose size restrictions on children. During Year 1 and Year 2 children should move to lined paper as they choose. Paper with differing spaces between the lines should be available.

Learning to maintain size and orientation

Learning to maintain an even size, slope orientation and spacing of letters and words is also helped by lined paper but the points listed above still apply. At first the child's whole effort goes into producing the correct movement patterns. Plain paper is required in order to give full scope for the child's individual strategy. Gradually the child aligns the letters more carefully and, through practice, begins to observe size, constancy and consistent spacing. Lined paper, introduced as this later process is beginning, can help evenness of handwriting to develop. The strategy for helping children with difficulties in the primary years consists of emphasising the lines. Often a middle line is added to set the top height for small letters. For children with severe difficulties the three lines are coloured and some children require squared paper. The lined and squared paper needs to be prepared on the basis of the child's average letter size when writing on plain paper.

Introducing a range of tools

The pencil is the best tool to use for early handwriting though the movement patterns should be practised in a wide range of media – paint, sand, air tracing, chalk, etc. A pencil bites into the paper enough to absorb small unskilled movements of the hand and fingers. Only clear movements shift the pencil, hence cleaner lines are made and the control needed to obtain the desired result is easier. Historically the major transfer point was from the pencil to the ink pen around seven or eight. Pens come in all shapes and sizes and the child with a less orthodox grip will need to experiment with a range of pens to find one s/he can control comfortably. The best modern strategy is to move from the pencil to the fibre tip but ink pens remain an option for older children should they wish to transfer. Biros are the hardest to control as the roller ball at the tip gives very little bite and is free to register all small muscle movements in any direction. Its lack of bite does make it, however, the fastest writing instrument and it is ideal for skilled handwriters, though surprisingly difficult to keep even when writing at speed.

Final phase

The final phase of handwriting development involves the continual speeding up of handwriting. Dutton (1989) has described how this moves from an average of 1.5 words per minute at age five to 18 words per minute at sixteen. This improvement is largely a practice effect and speed gains continue to be made at secondary school. Speed of writing is a reflection of a deep skill and 'being a slow writer' who misses or avoids recording opportunities is a matter for support and assistance rather than criticism and social pressure. There is little that can be done about skill development in this area as the child's handwriting patterns and habits are well set before speed becomes an educational issue.

Handwriting and whole body movement come together in the context of the body position which is required to write. A stable base is needed with a chair a third of the height of the child and a table a half of the child's height. The surface should slope gently towards the child; rare nowadays. The paper should slope at the same angle as the child's arm. Once a poor writing posture is established from whatever cause, it is difficult to alter. This alone can affect writing speed, distort letters and lead to fatigue or pain to the writer.

Drawing

From a motor perspective drawing involves the ability to make the basic geometric shapes and is thus complete at six years. This goes some way to explain why some children who experience significant problems with handwriting are described by parents and teachers as 'good at drawing'. This is a form of written expression which they are able to perform and from which they may derive pleasure. A cartoon format is often favoured or the lines may be 'feathered' rather than clearly defined. This latter adaptation to accommodate poor pencil control can be attractive in drawing but is inappropriate for handwriting.

A major developmental goal centres on drawing a person, beginning with the face and head and moving into the periphery, hands and fingers, towards the end of the process. Drawing involves many aspects other than motor control and is therefore not dealt with in detail here.

Handwriting and drawing

Developmental milestones

15 mths	picks up small objects between finger and thumb;
1 yr 6 mths	scribbles, holding the 'crayon' in the palm of the hand;
2 yrs	imitates in drawing horizontal, vertical and circular strokes and scribbles in circles and straight lines;
2 yrs 6 mths	imitates a circle; imitates a V;

3 yrs	copies a cross, a T and an H;
3 yrs 6 mths	draws a person with head, eyes, nose, mouth and legs;
4 yrs	copies a Y;
	drawing of a person now includes a trunk;
4 yrs 6 mths	drawing of a person now includes arms;
5 yrs	can now copy all the letters including a K and E;
	copies a square and then a triangle;
6 yrs	drawing of a person now has hands;
6 yrs 6 mths	copies a diamond;
7 yrs	size of handwriting approaches the general standard.

Activities to support the development of handwriting

Activities to establish movement patterns
- air tracing beginning with circular movements;
- copy whole arm movement patterns on a chalk board;
- use a brush to paint employing all varieties of whole arm movement. Initially the child is learning about the trace that their arm movements leave. Use an easel. Paint all the letters in large brush strokes before drawing them. Painting is underused in the early stages of writing;
- talk through all movements – up, down, round, across, stop, start, circle, left, right, forwards and backwards, clockwise, anticlockwise. Working on a vertical surface makes these directions easier for young children;
- parallel movement patterns with music and rhymes;
- draw a line through various mazes and pathways. These can require the whole range of movements – circular, wavy, zig-zag, sudden changes of direction, etc. Start with wide and then decrease to narrow pathways;
- dot-to-dot drawing going through simple continuous patterns to individual shapes.

Activities to develop wrist, hand and finger strength and skills
- finger and hand painting in any medium;
- finger rhymes putting firm pressure on the fingers;
- sticking coloured shapes on each finger and finger puppets;
- sand tracing with the fingers;
- palm and finger activity with dough, plasticine and clay;
- pull string, cord, wool, ribbon, etc. (wet and dry) through the fingers;
- all craft activities;
- pick-up-sticks game;
- use different strengths of peg on the side of a can;
- peg board patterns – eventually build in a race element;
- identifying objects in a feely bag;
- touch each finger in turn with the thumb. Start very slowly then turn into a race.

For many years, in the speech and language therapy profession, the speech disorder described as 'developmental verbal dyspraxia' has proved to be controversial. Arguments have surrounded not only the nature of the problem, but also its very existence. The term 'dyspraxia', or 'apraxia', as it is sometimes called, was originally used with reference to the adult population.

Much discussion has ranged around whether the severe speech problems experienced by some children mirrors those seen in adults. Increasingly, therapists are in agreement as to the developmental nature of the impairment (as discussed in Chapter 2), although full agreement on its clinical presentation has yet to be reached.

Much of the disagreement among speech and language therapists has been focused on the way in which the term developmental verbal dyspraxia (DVD) has been used to describe children whose problems appear to be very different. This has been based on the two main theoretical approaches used in relation to DVD.

Box 4.8   *Theoretical approaches*
A disorder of motor planning/programming
Edwards (1984) described DVD as 'an impairment of sensory processing and in particular of proprioceptive input, with an ensuing failure to programme, to organise and to carry out movements necessary for expressive speech'.

A linguistic/phonological impairment
Crary (1984) described DVD as 'a breakdown in the spatial/ temporal properties of movements, which cannot be explained by direct sensory-motor pathology'.

Exponents of the first theory would view DVD as purely a motor problem, resulting from the planning and programming of movements needed for speech. Those adhering to the second theory, however, would view the difficulty as part of a language disorder affecting development of the child's sound system. Disagreement on which theory should be adopted has been overcome by therapists taking a more pragmatic view, based on experience and an increasingly greater understanding of the condition. They now accept that problems stem from both viewpoints.

A useful working definition of the condition would be:

> Developmental verbal dyspraxia (or 'verbal dyspraxia', as it is more commonly called) is a condition where the child has difficulty in making and coordinating the precise movements which are used in the production of spoken language, although there is no damage to muscles or nerves.

So, verbal dyspraxia is characteristically a disorder in which speech is severely affected and language less so. Equally, some children are unfortunate enough to have almost all of the characteristics of the condition while others exhibit just a few.

The characteristics of verbal dyspraxia

Difficulty in control of the speech apparatus

The term 'speech apparatus' is used to include all those parts of our body involved in making and coordinating the precise movements necessary for accurate speech production (see Fig. 4.2).

- the jaw;
- the lips;
- the tongue;
- the soft palate, the part of our mouth which goes up and down when we say 'ah'. It is a 'fleshy' extension of the hard palate (roof of the mouth) which closes off our nose space from our mouth space, an action needed for sucking, blowing, swallowing and speaking;
- the larynx (the voice box);
- the muscles used to control breathing for speech;
- the muscles used for facial expression may also be involved.

Difficulty in making speech sounds

The child can only make a very limited number of sounds and this may include both consonants and vowels. A child with a severe verbal dyspraxia aged four and a half to five may still only have three to four consonant sounds and one or two vowels. Also, the ability to imitate adults at the single sound level may be limited.

Difficulty in sequencing sounds and sequencing sounds to make a word

Apparently simple sequences of the same sound such as b-b-b may be difficult. Sequences involving changes from one consonant to another such as b-d-g present even greater difficulties. The most complex sequences, those used in words with consonant–vowel combinations, are enormously difficult for the child. He will omit sounds or substitute other sounds and sometimes have a 'favourite articulation', where he uses one sound consonant or vowel in almost every word he says.

Difficulty in sequencing sounds for words in sentences

Even if a child can manage to pronounce single words with a degree of accuracy, once he attempts to sequence for words in sentences, he may become unintelligible.

Difficulty with feeding

Many of the children, as discussed in the section on feeding, are reported to have experienced problems with sucking, chewing, and moving on to solids and multitextured food. Parents often describe them as slow, messy or lazy eaters. A small number of children will continue to experience difficulties which, as they grow older, become increasingly unacceptable to their peers and adults with whom they have contact (teachers, dinner ladies).

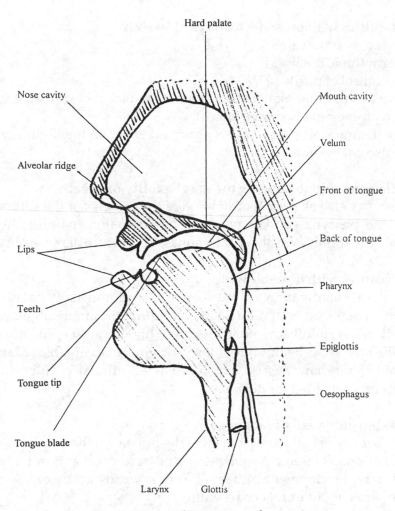

Labels on figure:
Hard palate
Nose cavity
Mouth cavity
Alveolar ridge
Velum
Front of tongue
Lips
Back of tongue
Teeth
Pharynx
Tongue tip
Epiglottis
Oesophagus
Tongue blade
Larynx
Glottis

Figure 4.2   The organs of speech

Difficulties with oral skills

'Oral dyspraxia is present when the child is unable to copy voluntary movements of the oral organs, i.e. tongue, lips, jaw and face on command or demonstration in the absence of attempts to articulate' (Milloy 1991). It is probable, although there is still discussion about this, that the lack of voluntary control so characteristic of oral dyspraxia, is linked with early and continuing feeding difficulties. These skills include tongue, lip, jaw and facial movements. Also dribbling may be an indicator of poor control of oral movement patterns.

Difficulty in controlling breathing and phonation (production of sound)

There may be poor coordination of the muscles used in respiration and voice production, so much so that the child may find it difficult to regulate his breathing or have enough breath for a complete sentence. He quite literally 'runs out of breath' and frequently his voice is weak or husky. Occasionally, an 'ingressive' (ingoing) airstream is used for speaking (we normally speak using an 'egressive' (outgoing) airstream). Volume can also be a problem.

Difficulties with prosodic features of speech
- rate of production;
- rhythmic quality;
- control of pitch;
- patterns of intonation (rise and fall of voice for expressiveness);
- volume can also be a problem.

These features of speech have a profound effect on intelligibility and can also change meaning.

Difficulties with balancing the nasal quality of speech
There may also be poor coordination of the muscles of the soft palate and the pharynx (throat) resulting in fluctuating nasality, hyper-nasality (excessive nasality) or hyponasality (insufficient nasality).

Difficulties with nose-blowing
The poor coordination of muscles of the mouth (soft palate and larynx) combined with difficulties controlling the airstream may well result in the child being unable to blow his/her nose. This not only implies a risk to health but is also socially unacceptable. Manipulation of the hand/tissue may present additional problems. (See Chapter 4.6, p. 61–2 for details.)

Slow development of language
The majority of children with verbal dyspraxia will have been slow to speak. Parents often describe their child as 'a good and quiet baby', with late development of babbling, first words and word joining. Problems continue and can be with:
- the length and complexity of their sentences;
- specific grammatical forms, e.g. verb tenses, plural forms and pronouns;
- the language of space and time, e.g. concepts such as behind, outside, next, etc. (see Chapter 4.1 and Chapter 5);
- more complex language associated with self-awareness, e.g. back of left knee, middle of forehead;
- word retrieval difficulties – the 'tip of the tongue' feeling;
- slow or poor development of social skills, particularly those associated with the protocols of language use and non-verbal communication, e.g. facial expression.

All or any of these may persist until seven or eight years (see Chapter 3). It is unusual, but they can persist into adolescence.

Therapists observe several other general characteristics of verbal dyspraxia:
- speech production is inconsistent. One attempt of the same word may be correct while a second may be incorrect;
- progress is extremely slow;
- the child very quickly becomes aware of his problems. Some children become so aware that they choose not to speak other than to their parents, i.e. become selectively mute.

Verbal dyspraxia – the cause or causes

To date the cause of verbal dyspraxia is not known, although it is thought most likely that the root of the problem is immature neural development. Children with verbal dyspraxia are sometimes from families where there is a history of speech delay or disorder. Speech and language therapists, who have worked for many years in one specific district, are familiar with these 'dynasties'.

Pembrey in Fletcher and Hall (1992) profiles a family where fifteen out of twenty-nine members, over three generations, had severe verbal dyspraxia, and two others, both young children, were of 'questionable status' (diagnosis not yet confirmed).

Preschoolers

The preschool child will have very different needs to one of school age. Speech and language therapists would always prefer to see the child sooner rather than later.

The profile of a two year old would typically be as follows:
- the child has no speech at all;
- he sometimes has poor verbal comprehension (the link between verbal dyspraxia and poor verbal comprehension is very complex and the subject of professional debate);
- he has feeding difficulties;
- he is having tantrums and showing signs of frustration or has completely withdrawn.

Feeding difficulties would alert the therapist that this child might have verbal dyspraxia, but until the child is willing to communicate verbally this will not be clear. The plan at this stage would be:

Box 4.9 *Action plan*
- to improve verbal comprehension;
- include child in a small early language group, as at this stage one-to-one therapy may be too pressured.

As the child progresses the aims of therapy would change to meet his needs.

Box 4.10 *Action plan*
- to address any feeding difficulties;
- to inhibit excessive dribbling (see feeding);
- to improve attention and listening skills;
- to learn the skills needed to communicate with others, e.g. turn-taking, making eye contact;
- to improve oral skills;
- to attempt making sounds, sound sequences and enjoying the experience;
- to practise a little and often in order to establish correct patterns of movement;
- to include parents in therapy as much as possible;
- to use a manual signing system or a visual (symbol) communication system.

Case study 1

Preschool

R was referred to speech and language therapy because he was 'not talking'. He was reported to have been rather slow in learning to walk and was a 'fussy' and 'faddy' eater. R was seen for assessment at age two years ten months when it was also noted he occasionally dribbled, was rather 'wet' around his mouth and had an open mouth posture. His parents were worried that as a baby he was very quiet and did not babble until seventeen to eighteen months. At age two years and ten months he sometimes used single words, but his preferred method of communication was through physical means – showing parents what he wanted by grabbing them or by gesture. R was not cooperative at first, so assessment was prolonged, but gradually a profile emerged indicating both motor and verbal dyspraxia.

He was found to have:

- poor oral skills: those already observed, plus there were no differentiated movements of his tongue and his palate was poorly coordinated;
- he was using a 'favourite articulation', 'ba', but was heard to use 'd' and a limited range of vowels;
- he was unable to sequence any sounds, but showed some knowledge of syllable structure;
- his verbal comprehension was slightly delayed for his age.

R attended therapy at the local clinic for a few months during which his verbal comprehension improved, but was referred to the local Child Development Centre, where he could receive more intensive help for both his speech and motor problems. Therapy was aimed at developing all motor skills, oral and general, and establishing a sound system (access to physiotherapy and occupational therapy was available). Initially, R needed an augmentative communication system and Makaton signing was introduced. R became a more outgoing little boy once he realised he could communicate more efficiently. His remaining feeding and dribbling problems were dealt with and R joined a local playgroup. As he progressed R's attention and social awareness improved and he became a cooperative but rather 'loud' little boy. His mother said he had a voice like a 'foghorn'! By age four and a half R was transferred back to the local clinic and at school entry, age five years, he was intelligible if the context was known. Good cooperation between clinic and school ensured that R's difficulties were understood and well managed. By six years eight months he was able to use a full range of speech sounds, had improved control over his voice and patterns of intonation and was intelligible.

R has remaining difficulties with spelling and motor organisation, but his school is continuing to provide extra help for these.

School-age children – management within the class/ therapy context

Therapists work in several different ways with mainstream schools – these are discussed in Chapter 3. These ways of working will only apply to those children who remain in a mainstream class, which is the majority. A minority will have their needs met in a Language Unit, which is a small class (usually eight to ten children) with a specialist teacher, therapist and full-time classroom assistant. These classes are usually attached to mainstream schools and are for children who have a range of severe speech and language impairments.

In a mainstream class, a child with dyspraxia will, most likely, be receiving his therapy from the therapist at the local health clinic and would have been assessed as a child with significant special needs. Much of the therapy for children with verbal dyspraxia, particularly that for 'motor programming', can only be carried out on a one-to-one or small group withdrawal basis. With appropriate training from the speech and language therapist, teachers, classroom assistants and therapy assistants can undertake this work. Other aspects of therapy, associated with specific language difficulties, phonological awareness, word retrieval, prosody and social skills, can be more easily integrated into everyday classroom activities. Inevitably also, there are other children in the class with special needs, who benefit from focused attention on these areas of learning.

Many of the approaches used with young children are also used with older children, but as they mature children are able to concentrate for longer periods and more easily understand aims of therapy. It is possible, therefore, to introduce more complex approaches and ideas.

Liaison with the classteacher

The classteacher will want to know:
- how best to communicate with the child, e.g. are signs needed;
- what idiosyncratic signs, sounds, words the child uses for basic requests such as toilet, drink, hurt, play, yes, no;
- how much the child understands;
- what specific work is being practised in therapy so that a programme can be followed in school;
- what therapy work can be integrated into the curriculum;
- should s/he correct the child or not;
- whether the child is likely to experience difficulties with reading, spelling and writing, and what approaches might be adopted to help (the educational psychologist and the occupational therapist would also need to be consulted).

To facilitate the development of the sound system

There are some general rules which apply to therapy used for the development of the child's sound system. For the acquisition of reliable and consistent production of sounds and sound sequences, the children need to have feedback through more than one sense. The three senses are visual, tactile and proprioceptive and ideally each integrates with the others to give effective feedback to the child:

- to make the sound 'visual', child and therapist (parent/teacher/ classroom assistant) may sit side by side, facing a large mirror so that they can easily see where the tongue position is in the mouth;
- to give proprioceptive feedback, the child's attention, for example, is drawn to the feel of the tongue against the gum ridge when making the 't' sound;
- use a straw to tickle the gum ridge or put chocolate spread (or other spread tolerated by the child) there to give a tactile stimulus of the appropriate position for the tongue. Note: great care must be taken in choosing spreads because of childhood allergies.

The aims of this type of therapy are always the same:

- to improve the accuracy and speed of articulatory movements;
- to unite these movements into coordinated sequences;
- to provide the child with a systematic yet flexible approach.

Oral skills work is often done simultaneously (see Chapter 4.6, p. 61).

The therapist would be using all or any combination of the following programmes/approaches, with this type of therapy.

The Nuffield Dyspraxia Programme

Many parents and teachers will already be familiar with this excellent programme which is used for improving the 'motor programming' aspects of verbal dyspraxia. It contains:

- an assessment section;
- basic motor work advice sheets;
- a therapy section;
- a comprehensive manual.

All the sounds used in the programme have visual symbols, and the system is comprehensive enough for parts of it to be used to suit a child's individual needs. It combines oral skills work with sound production and sequencing. This enables the therapist to extend the child's skills at several levels simultaneously. Repetition is used to help achieve and establish success, and frequent exercise to build up patterns. It also enables the child to use these skills eventually in spontaneous speech.

Metaphon

This approach teaches children to become aware of the features of sounds, e.g. noisy/quiet (referring to voiced/voiceless speech sounds), and how they contrast with one another in words to change meaning.

Letterland

Many teachers are familiar with the Letterland Scheme but Letterland can be used in different ways to support children with verbal dyspraxia:

- a 'Hairy Hat Man' party, and only the quiet (voiceless sounds) people in Letterland are invited. The children have to guess who can go to the party;
- play a 'pairs game' with Letterland cards – find two noisy or two quiet people for a pair;
- Letterland dominoes – only noisy or quiet people can go together.

At an earlier stage, the concepts of noisy/quiet could be included in music sessions, and general class routine – 'who are noisy people and who are quiet people'. Later on when the child is at a stage of identifying noisy/quiet sounds in words, it can be linked to general 'phonological awareness' activities going on in class, which focuses on the children learning about the structure of words.

Cuing

For some children with verbal dyspraxia cuing can be another helpful prop to their speech sound learning. The manual gestures used represent the movements and positions required to produce consonants and vowels, and the cuing takes place near to or along the side of the face.

Signing

This may not be needed with all children, but acts as a useful means of supporting verbal communication. Makaton and Signed English are the most commonly used manual signing systems. If a child has become selectively mute, there are symbol systems such as Makaton and Rebus symbols which can also be used.

Using reading to reinforce therapy

Once a child has successfully begun to read and write, aspects of speech production can be supported. His/her speech is always going to be clearer when reading aloud, because it is not a creative process. The child does not have to:

- formulate syntax;
- select vocabulary;
- sequence words;
- use intonation, etc.;
- interact with another person.

The child has to:

- match the word he is reading to one already known;
- use visual representation for clues as to pronunciation once that specific stage of reading has been achieved;
- segment and attempt new words which have visual representations.

Case study 2

So what might a therapist be asking a parent/teacher/ancillary to do? An example is S who is five years eight months old, in a mainstream class, and has a Statement of Educational Needs. He has been receiving help for his verbal dyspraxia since age three years and eight months and is currently working on expanding the range of consonant sounds he can say, practising them in sequences and with vowels. At the same time his oral skills still need help and he has poor breath control for speech – he either speaks too loudly or too quietly. The school has:

- acquired a large mirror;
- built up an oral skills box;
- found a quiet place for him to work with the classroom assistant.

They are following the therapist's programme:

- look in the mirror – sit side by side;
- tongue exercises to improve elevation in and outside the mouth, moving tongue inside and outside mouth and locating positions around mouth and inside mouth using any of the 'spreads' from the oral skills box;
- blowing bubbles to improve breath control and incorporate a sequence of movements;
- practise single sounds, d and g; the normal developmental sequence of sounds is usually followed unless a child finds he can say another sound more easily. S is being taught to lift the front and then the back of his tongue;
- these single sounds are incorporated into sequences, e.g. d-d-d/g-g-g combined with other sounds he can say, e.g. b-d/ b-g/b-d-g. These are then combined with vowels boo-dee/ boo-gee, etc.;
- S is learning about long/short sounds in music and has further practice in a small group.

S's programme is updated on a weekly basis.

Language work

Children with verbal dyspraxia are likely to experience difficulties with certain aspects of language as outlined earlier in this chapter. Teachers can help considerably by focusing on these in class.

The language of space and time

Vocabulary such as first, second, next, last, before, after, beginning, end, behind, between, outside, inside, further from, nearer to and so on, can be integrated into:

- the language associated with general classroom organisation;
- the sequence of events in the day;
- the sequence of a task;
- lining up;
- circle time (taking turns);

- PE (the language needed for all PE tasks);
- music and movement;
- maths;
- project work;
- organised games.

Grammar

The understanding of verb tense is closely associated with an understanding of time generally. Work on organisation within a time frame such as happens in a classroom helps considerably. Specific aspects of verb tense need to be taught as the child will also have had problems pronouncing word endings, e.g. 'the cat run<u>s</u> fast'. This can be included in written class work as well as following a specific programme from the therapist.

Pronouns are best taught in context, particularly personal pronouns. They link in well with a topic such as 'myself', and any games where turn-taking and gender are needed, e.g. Je M'Habille, and circle games – give it to 'her', 'him'; it's 'hers', 'his', etc. Words which refer to relationships within families e.g. brother/sister may be hard for the children to understand.

Length and complexity of sentences

Children with verbal dyspraxia often use short sentences because typically they have been unable to pronounce long sentences which require complex sequences of sounds. Once the children begin to read they become more aware of longer sentences. Also they will learn from discussing topics in class how to phrase more complex sentences. Their own written language can also be used as a means of expanding spoken language.

Word retrieval difficulties

These are frequently the result of poor 'phonological representation', when the child was learning the words. The child has filed away his own version of the word, using different sounds and sound sequences to others. This is helped by intensive work on all aspects of 'phonological awareness', which will improve the child's knowledge of word structure and word families.

Difficulties with prosody

The language needed to understand these aspects of speech are terms frequently used in class, e.g. up, down, fast, slow, faster, slower, faster than, slower than, high, higher, higher than, low, lower than, rising, falling, loud, quiet.

Music, among other subjects, provides an excellent means through which these concepts can be taught, by:

- making loud/quiet sounds with a variety of instruments;
- making sounds go up and down using chime bars;
- drums are a wonderful means of learning about fast/slow;
- rhythm is experienced through joining a known tune with instruments;

- combinations of any of these concepts can be achieved with any of the instruments, e.g. loud and slow, quiet and rising (going up) and so on. Specific vocal work would need to be undertaken in close collaboration with the therapist and at this stage tasks can be incorporated into singing and drama.

Social skills

The skills of conversation:
- what to say;
- when to say it;
- how to say it

are learned at the earliest age. In their first year of life, even before spoken language develops, babies learn the art of 'give' and 'take' in communication. It is well documented (Conti-Ramsden 1987)) that mothers respond less to babies who do not acquire language in the usual way. This is not deliberate but, in fact, sets up a pattern which continues as the child develops and meets new people, adults and children. So, by the time the child enters school, his social skills are often poor.

To date, for most children with verbal dyspraxia, the adult has been considered as a 'reluctant listener', but, of course, by now the child has become a 'reluctant speaker'.

To become more effective listeners we need to be aware of the rules of conversational interaction. The following are some of the more important:

Listener	*Speaker*
A listening posture	Eye contact
Body position	Repair of grammar/speech
Increased eye contact	Checking response of listener
Turn taking	Turn taking
Commenting	Body position
Appropriate interruptions/ interjections	Sequencing the topic
	Knowing when to stop

Useful tips on how to deal with a child with verbal dyspraxia

- use other children to help – they can often tell you what has been said;
- don't ask for repetitions as you'll probably get a different version;
- use pictures or symbols as a resource to facilitate communication;
- repetition and clarification can be undertaken so that the responsibility passes to the child by:
  - picking out the words you have or think you have heard and feeding them back to the child, e.g. Are you talking about Mum? Did she go to the x?

- keep listening for recognisable words and keep feeding them back before too much more is said.

By using these strategies the conversation is being maintained, as is eye contact and listening posture.

- use a home/school book to get as much information about what has happened/is happening/will happen, in the child's life;
- don't forget to encourage natural gestures, if a signing system is not being used;
- encourage the use of non-verbal cues;
- help the child maintain the sequence of information. This reduces 'loading' on his brain by giving him time to concentrate on speech production, sentence formulation, word selection, and any other techniques suggested by the therapist he ought to be practising;
- be positive, it helps build confidence and enables the child to become more effective at monitoring his own performance.

All of these strategies can be practised in games, play situations and social skills games and activities.

Class opportunities for language work

- news time;
- listening to stories;
- turn-taking games;
- working in small groups (supervised);
- writing stories;
- re-telling stories;
- reporting back on project work;
- talking about art work;
- plus other activities mentioned on p. 52–3.

Development of speech and language

Developmental milestones

1 mth	cries, smiles, gurgles;
3 mths	listens, coos, responds;
6 mths	laughs, chuckles, squeals, babbles in syllables;
9 mths	listens carefully, attention seeking, longer babbles, understands 'no';
1 yr	knows name, understands 20–60 words, babbles tunefully incessantly, *first words* appear;
15 mths	uses jargon up to 50 words, understands 150–200 words;
18 mths	long jargon – like conversations with increased use of recognised words, beginning of word linking, e.g. Daddy gone;
2 yrs	uses 50+ recognisable words – understands more, repeats what people say (echolalia), speech unclear;
3 yrs	large vocabulary, intelligible to strangers, repeats sentence containing six or seven syllables. Asks questions, simple conversations;

4 yrs   speech grammatically correct, completely intelligible, some immaturity of sounds used, enjoys jokes. Repeats sentences with 12–13 syllables;

5 yrs   speech fluent, grammatically conventional, sounds correct except for confusions of 's', 'f', 'th' and others such as 'spr';

6 yrs   as above – speech sound system fully developed and mature.

Sound system

This chart shows the normal developmental sequence of sounds:

Age	Lip	Tongue (front)	Tongue (back)
2 yrs	m	n	
	p b	t d	
	w		
2–2.5 yrs	m	n	ng
	p b	t d	(k g)
	w		h
2.5–3 yrs	m	n	ng
	p f b	t d	k g
	w	s y	h
		(l)	
3.5–4 yrs	m	n	ch ng
	p b	t d	k g
	f v	s z	sh j h
	w	l y	
4.5 yrs+	m	t n d	ch ng
	p b	s z y	k g
	f v(th)	l r	h
	w		

Section 6: Feeding and eating

The movements of eating and drinking follow a clear developmental sequence from the reflex, suckle/swallowing to sophisticated voluntary chewing. One of the many characteristics of verbal dyspraxia is difficulty with feeding.

Most children have strong components of reflex patterns when they first start suckling and when they later progress to early chewing. However, even when their movements are strongly influenced by reflexes, they have a range of movement options available to them which allows them to cope with variations in food presentation and utensils.

The children gradually establish voluntary control over the range of eating and drinking patterns required for increasingly complex food, so by the age of two years, they have mastered the basis of mature eating patterns. It only remains for them to establish even finer control over the patterns to gain clean, sophisticated eating and drinking.

Dyspraxic babies have difficulties establishing a controlled range of oral movements:

- they have a reduced adaptability of their oral movement patterns for variations in food presentation and utensils;
- the reduced adaptability means they may experience more frequent, unpleasant choking or gagging. This leads to a reduction in their willingness to experiment when eating and drinking;
- they may retain a modified suckle/swallow pattern involving squashing and swallowing food, which may suffice to soften and break up a considerable range of foods, except meat;
- they may have a limited range of control of lip and tongue movements, which will maintain the reliance on squash/swallow movement patterns for dealing with food;
- their limited movements mean they experiment less with their mouths and do not discover the full range of what their mouths can do;
- their limited control means they do not experiment with sensations and do not discover the full range of sensations that their mouths can tolerate.

In addition, children with oral/verbal dyspraxia frequently have a more generalised dyspraxia and this further interferes with feeding because of delayed hand-to-mouth coordination.

Box 4.11   *Problems – delayed hand to mouth development*
- the baby experiments less with mouth movements because he cannot easily access his mouth and place food/object where he wants it;
- the baby experiences a smaller range of textures, tastes, temperatures than usual, because he is taking a smaller range of things to his mouth;
- there is a disruption of the usual process of desensitisation, whereby the baby reduces the sensitivity of his own mouth, by feeling, handling, inspecting a whole range of things orally.

A frequent characteristic of a child with oral dyspraxia is strong food preference and such children are often described as extremely fussy or faddy. Any food that has a smooth consistency and can be dealt with by the squash/swallow pattern is enjoyed; however, so are some other 'lumpy' and 'crunchy' foods, which might be construed as being difficult to eat. Certain 'lumpy' food is enjoyed by children because they quickly soften or dissolve and can then be dealt with easily by the squash/swallow pattern.

Certain children with dyspraxia who have mastered some chewing, may also enjoy dry finger foods, e.g. fish fingers, chips and peas. The texture and temperature can be experienced through the hands before it goes in the mouth and then pieces are usually placed to the side ready for instant chewing.

Box 4.12   *Examples of preferred food*
- yoghurt/fromage frais/angel delight, etc.;
- Ready Brek;
- custard;
- potato;
- biscuits (not those containing 'lumps', e.g. chocolate chip cookies or those containing two textures, e.g. jammy dodgers;
- baby foods;
- Wotsits;
- Skips;
- chocolate.

The least tolerated foods for children with dyspraxia are multitextured food such as would be presented at a main meal, e.g. meat and two vegetables and gravy or mixed vegetables in a sauce with rice. These are presented on a spoon or fork, which gives the child little information on texture or temperature before it enters the mouth. The mixture of lumps and liquid requires the highest level of sensory tolerance and most sophisticated oral control to ensure liquid is swallowed, lumps are chewed, saliva is mixed, larger lumps are stored, dribble is controlled and debris is cleared. The child with dyspraxia frequently lacks the oral sophistication required by the 'normal' adult meal.

Working on feeding

The assessment of a young child with oral dyspraxia may result in a range of problems being identified. The toddler may:
- be a competent eater, but fussy and faddy;
- be stuck at one of the early feeding stages (usually squash/swallow) and mother is liquidising foods or he may be a child who has a clear preference for foods such as yoghurt/biscuits;
- have oral sensitivity, so much so that he cannot tolerate very much in his mouth;
- have extremely anxious parents who have been through 'hell' in terms of feeding;
- be anxious and sensitive himself about food.

Oral sensitivity
The main aim is to decrease oral sensitivity by moving from smooth food which is tolerated to multitextured food. This process sometimes means combining foods that one would not usually consider as tasteful or acceptable.

Box 4.13   *Action plan*
- always start with food the child knows he can chew, e.g. crisps;
- combine something with it that has a different texture, e.g. cheese sauce;
- juggle as much as possible with different types of food;
- allow finger feeding, food touching;
- be totally convinced and convincing about the combinations of foods;
- persist in offering new foods over a long period of time to establish familiarity;
- encourage food play, e.g. food preparation, non-mealtime messy food play.

Progression through developmental stages

Paradoxically one of the best bridges from smooth to multitextured food is using convenience or economy foods. This advocacy of 'junk' food may not be comfortable for parents who will aim to give their children the best quality diet.

An example of an economy choice over a quality choice is fish fingers.

Economy fish fingers	*Good quality fish fingers*
contain 'mashed' fish	contain flaked fish
make easy bolus	not easy to make a bolus
require minimal chewing	need a lot of chewing and pushing round mouth
leave no debris	leave debris

The same qualities apply to reconstituted meat roll vs a slice of chicken.

Box 4.14   *Some general guidelines for parents*
- attempt changes at snack time first and then try a main meal, it is less stressful and more achievable;
- use only two types of food at first and then increase the number;
- use one food type that is going to create a lot of debris;
- make sure the other food type is smooth/sticky/clogging, e.g. mashed potato, sauce;
- finger feed with the 'lumpy' food, i.e. the one which will create debris;
- follow up with a mouthful of the other food type using a spoon, which will collect up the debris from the 'lumpy' food;
- a sip of juice after each mouthful may be helpful.

Extremes of temperature

These are not well tolerated and need to be introduced gradually. The following ideas are useful:

> **Box 4.15** *Action plan*
> - take the yoghurt out of the fridge half an hour before time;
> - pop the ice-cream into the microwave;
> - avoid cold drinks straight from the fridge (not the fizzy sort) – take out early or put in the microwave;
> - dip tolerated warm food into cold food.

Utensils

Dyspraxic children frequently have difficulty using utensils, because of their poor organisation, poor coordination, poor oral skills and inability to cross the mid-line. A whole range of modified utensils is available but parents would need to be advised by their therapist which would be the most appropriate to help overcome their child's feeding difficulties.

Food play

This is most helpful for those children who are sensitive to:
- anything on their hands: this could be paint, plasticine, water, as well as food;
- taking anything to their mouths.

> **Box 4.16** *Action plan*
> Promote desensitisation-awareness of food:
> - draw pictures in food and other messy food stuffs;
> - while doing this, children put their hands in their mouths, on their faces, hair, clothes, etc.; this gradually decreases sensitivity;
> - play games where you put food of different textures on arms, hands, nose, ears, cheeks, etc. (be prepared for the child to return the compliment!);
> - messy eaters need similar games but with a different outcome, 'Oh look where the food is now.'

Oral skills work

Therapists have an 'oral skills box' which contains a wide selection of equipment to improve oral skills, which can be used by parents and teachers with appropriate guidance.

Box 4.17   *The oral skills box*

Item	Possible use
Milky bar spread	For licking exercises
Marshmallow spread	
Peanut butter spreads	
Chocolate spread	
Sweets	
100s and 1000s	
Icing sugar	
Marmite	
Ice lollies	
Glue spatulas*	
Rice paper	
Sugar strands	
Sugar confetti shapes	
Gummed paper/stars	
Candles	For blowing and breath
Bubble mixture and	direction exercises
different size bubble-	
blowers and bubble	
rings	
Blow football	
Straws – different sizes	
and shapes	
Carnival blowers	
Whistlers	
Cotton wool	
Tissue paper	
Ping pong balls	
Lipstick	For mouth shape exercises
Mirror	
Fine brushes	For desensitization

*Glue spatulas – easy to lick off the spread, easy to apply the spread where you want on the child's mouth. Try to use spatulas that are a different colour from those actually used for the glue.

This is not a definitive list as there are increasingly many interesting and varied items which can be used for oral skills work – a visit to the local Early Learning Centre will testify to this!

Nose blowing

To help with nose blowing:
- get the child to identify where his/her nose is on their face, eyes open/eyes shut. Look and feel – look in a mirror;

- demonstrate to child how air comes out of your mouth and also out of your nose. Look, see, feel;
- talk about nostrils and how air can come down each separately or together. Look, see, feel;
- use a small mirror and hold under child's nose to show how it is possible to mist it by air from the nose;
- practise this with one nostril, then the other;
- practise blowing through mouth 'little' blows and 'big' blows so child experiences the difference;
- then try little and big blows through nostrils separately;
- at this stage, with a tissue between your thumb and index finger, gently grasp the child's nose. Close off one nostril with pressure from your thumb and ask the child to blow down the other nostril while moving your index finger backward and forward against the side of the open nostril. Then change nostrils;
- the child then needs to have practice coordinating holding the tissue in the right place and closing off each nostril separately. This takes a high degree of organisation when combined with the act of directing air down the nose.

Feeding and eating

Developmental milestones
Suckle/swallow
This reflex is present at birth and begins to diminish from six to eight weeks onwards. From nine months it is not present on smooth food.

Squash/swallow
A protrusion/retraction movement where the tongue is flat and squashes food against the roof of the mouth. This is one of the patterns used between three and eighteen months on smooth food, six to eighteen months on multitextured mash, and six to twenty-four months on lumps. Squash and swallow is rarely the only oral movement pattern available to the child. It is usually seen in combination with experimental lip/tongue and jaw movements on the food being eaten.

The front munch
Where lumps are 'chewed' between the front teeth with small vertical jaw movements, occurs for a short period around 6 months as the only way to manage lumps.

The primitive chew
A primitive stereotyped rhythmical close and release pattern on lumps falling between the molar gums or teeth, takes over from the front munch at about seven months, with rhythm and jaw modifications soon appearing.

Suck centre/chew side

This is a transitional oral pattern present between five to six months onwards. During this period children use head tilting and/or their fingers to achieve transfer of food, but they gradually develop the ability of the tongue to transfer food laterally.

Diagonal chew

This is a developmental stage between the primitive chew and mature chewing. The diagonal jaw movements are made in association with evolving lateral tongue movements. By fifteen months diagonal movements are smooth and well coordinated, and at twenty-four or more months fully circular rotary movements occur in association with a complete range of tongue movements.

Lip movements

During this period (birth to twenty-four months) the range and control of movements develop. Initially, voluntary movements may be limited to rounding for sucking, but more movement options quickly develop: straightening and tightening of the top lip to assist in removing food from a spoon, tucking in the bottom lip for lip biting, lateral movements associated with lateral movement of food in the mouth, to full mobility and closure coinciding with the fully mature rotary chewing pattern.

Chapter 5

Living with Dyspraxia

The developmental perspective has shown us that there is no statistical cut-off point which could define whether a child was dyspraxic or not. Motor coordination becomes a problem when limited skills are causing anxiety, distress or frustration to a child and his/her parents, and are affecting learning and behaviour. The different ways in which motor impairment can reveal itself between individuals and over situations often makes it hard for adults always to understand and to be sympathetic.

Some puzzles

- Why, if he can pick up a cup and drink when he is thirsty, can't (won't, implied) he do it when I ask him to?
  The first action is automatic, triggered by presence of cup and perception of thirst. The second action is a directed, voluntary action to be planned.
- He is only five and can stand on his head, why can't he control a pencil?
  Balance and gross-motor skills are much better developed than fine-motor skills.
- It can't be a motor problem, he runs well, he just can't sit still.
  Dynamic movement is much better developed than steady balance and control.

It is easy as an adult to assume that if a child can do one action s/he should be able to carry out a different related action and to conclude that s/he is being lazy, stubborn or defiant. As early as 1937 Orton described children who were delayed in reaching developmental goals for movement and had great difficulty with complex movements such as sequences of movement and the coordination of movements. It was found that these children were perceived by adults to be: lazy, careless, of low ability and that participation in competitive activities resulted in a 'sense of inferiority'. Unfortunately, these perceptions are still only too common in the 1990s.

Studies of children over time (longitudinal studies) show that motor problems which receive no therapeutic attention persist into adolescence and adulthood (Cermak 1985). Work by Chesson *et al.* (1991) showed that seventeen of the thirty-two families who had children receiving occupational therapy had recognised that there was a problem before the age of four, thirteen of them before any professionals had become involved.

Parents say:

> 'We, as parents, knew that there was something wrong very early on . . . he felt floppy . . . he didn't interact as well as his older sister had done.'

But:

> 'He can't be mentally handicapped: "he's got a naughty eye," said a friend, and he had.'

Some children in the Chesson *et al.* study had received help before they started school but often this focused on only one aspect of their child's functioning, such as speech, and their parents felt that the full extent of the problem had not been recognised.

Difficulties with the development of communication can be crucial during the early years as social life with parents, relatives, other adults and children can all be adversely affected. The frustration of not being understood can result in temper tantrums and aggressive behaviour towards other children. In this situation it is all too easy to focus upon the behaviour and not address the underlying problem: the need to communicate.

Parents say:

> 'At playgroup he could not ask for a turn with a toy – so he pushed and grabbed. The supervisor kept telling me he was naughty.'

> 'You know who your friends are when your toddler flings bricks at anyone who approaches.'

If intelligible speech is a long-term goal then signs or natural gestures can ease the mutual frustration of a parent and child who are unable to communicate effectively.

Parents say:

> 'The joy of his first sentence as he stumped in pulling his sister along and announcing "Us wants biscuits."'

Parents may be aware that their dyspraxic child is slower to move about and explore the environment. Even within a toddler group the children may get left behind as the others move around, play

Preschool years

Box 5.1

Language becomes a substitute for action as children develop:
- the ability to understand what is said to them;
- the ability to express their needs.

For example, a child with limited language might be found climbing on the kitchen cabinets in search of a biscuit. A child with language would have the option of asking a taller person to get the biscuit tin down.

If language does not develop very well, children are put under pressure to conform without the ability to understand and to behave as is expected. The result can be tantrums, aggressive behaviour or other difficult behaviour which become the focus of attention rather than the underlying language problem. This is described by professionals as abnormal language development leading to disruption in the development of behavioural control.

(Baker and Cantwell 1987)

with the toys and begin to interact with each other. When they walk the movement patterns may appear different or awkward and compensatory movements (e.g. movements of the free arm when doing a task with the other) can make them appear 'odd'. Parents may be quite embarrassed about how others perceive their child. Frequent falls may result in more bruises than even most toddlers acquire, with the attendant worries about whether 'people' will think the child is being abused. The differences can intrude even during pleasurable outings:

> A group of mothers with their preschool children were out for a walk on a summer afternoon. They approached a stile and all but one child managed to negotiate the stile with minimum help.
>
> P stood rigid and seemed unable to plan which bit of her body to move first in order to carry out the complex sequence of movements which was needed in order to climb the stile. 'In the end we just lifted her over.'

Getting children up and dressed in the morning can be tense, especially when there is a time limit. Most dyspraxic children will find it hard to acquire the self-help skills which are involved in dressing:
- a poor body image may affect the decision about which bits of clothing fit which bits of the body and which way round they go;
- limited fine-motor skills make the fastening of buttons, zips or the tucking in of T-shirts difficult;
- sequencing and planning difficulties can make it hard to decide which order to put on clothes – pants outside trousers like Batman.

It is only the most patient of parents who will not show frustration and resort to dressing their child on many occasions.

In the same way that getting up and going to bed can become stressful moments for parent and child, frustrations may also focus around mealtimes. There may be a history of early feeding problems (see Chapter 4.6) because of poor coordination of the mechanisms for chewing and swallowing and so eating may be associated with tension and anxieties which persist into childhood. The early chewing problems may influence a child to be unambitious in trying new foods with different textures. A child who does not/will not eat what the rest of the family eats may be hard to accommodate. At the age when most children have mastered the complicated art of feeding themselves, the dyspraxic child may have difficulties finding their mouth accurately, chewing neatly and using two utensils in a coordinated way. Accidents such as spilling drinks, knocking things off the table, food leaping off the plate, become less tolerated as a child gets older and some families may be reluctant to take the child out to eat whether with friends, relatives or to a restaurant.

Long before starting school the dyspraxic child will have had experiences of being frustrated during their interactions with the physical environment. Other children, even younger siblings, may be able to run faster or further, pedal and steer the tricycle, open doors more efficiently, build Lego models better – the list can be endless and the child is already at risk of developing low self-esteem.

What parents noted as different

Area of difficulty	Percentage reported
Speech difficulties	50%
Running	55%
Jumping	52%
Hopping	61%
Late to develop a mature grasp	50%
Balancing and bike-riding	68%
Throwing and catching	90% (Chesson et al. 1991)

Of the thirty-two families in the Chesson et al. study, fourteen were unaware that their child had difficulties before they started school and a few were reluctant to acknowledge that there was a problem when the teacher attempted to discuss their child's progress. In contrast, five families were aware of a problem and it was the teacher who denied that there was a problem in school.

Chesson et al. quote a typical mismatch of perceptions:

Mother: 'He is shy, a loner who wants to please.'

Teacher: (who had observed him sitting alone during free play but knew he had a good vocabulary and assumed that he was an able child) 'He is lazy and underachieving.'

The primary school

Parents did comment that early identification had been helpful when it provided an opportunity for them and the occupational therapist to explain the child's difficulties to the teacher when they started school. Identification of the problem can also lead to some positive experiences once a child has started school:

> 'The teacher seems to understand his problems more and is trying to do all she can to help.'

> 'He is pleased that people realise that it's not his fault, that he's not doing it on purpose.'

In the Chesson *et al.* study the educational psychologist had played a key role in the identification of most of the children, but children had seldom been referred to the educational psychologist before starting school. Once the children are in school the referral to the educational psychologist seldom highlights motor problems as the key area of concern and the central role of these difficulties may only become apparent as the assessment proceeds. Referrals to the educational psychologist usually occur for one or more of the following reasons:

- learning difficulties with handwriting or reading;
- behavioural response to the difficulties which they are experiencing in the classroom: withdrawn, apathetic, loss of interest, a distracter who plays the clown, hostile, aggressive;
- concern about peer relationships;
- psychosomatic symptoms, e.g. bedwetting, stomach aches.

The dyspraxic child in the classroom

In the Chesson *et al.* study twenty-seven of the thirty-two children were receiving some learning support within school and for fifteen of these the focus was upon the basic skills of reading, writing, spelling. Although the main reason for referral to outside agencies such as the educational psychologist is most often for learning difficulties, other comments are common on the referral forms or are mentioned during consultation.

Common teacher perceptions include:
- He won't sit still.
- Why is his handwriting so awful?
- He wanders around.
- His books are such a mess.
- He swings on his chair and falls off.
- He can never find his place in a book.
- A real fidget, especially during story time.
- He never wants to paint or model.
- The class clown.
- He's so slow getting changed for PE

- He often leaves out complete pages in his books.
- He cannot keep his files in order and loses his work.
- He's always bumping into people in line – this irritates them.

Children with dyspraxia can, of course, have abilities which span the whole range from exceptionally able to significant learning difficulties. However, it may not always be easy to assess their abilities because of the difficulties they experience with making a response if their speech and language is difficult to follow and they have problems with the fine-motor skills required for drawing or writing. Whatever the ability level of a dyspraxic child, s/he is likely to experience problems which will affect responses in the classroom and progress with core curriculum subjects.

Handwriting and the dyspraxic child

For dyspraxic children handwriting problems are the most common area of teacher concern in the classroom.

In his study of primary school children in Leeds, Professor Alexander (1992) found that children aged seven to eight years spent 33 per cent of their time doing written work of some kind, so by Year 3 a child who experiences significant difficulties with recording is also bound to experience significant frustration in the classroom. Some of the 'wandering' and 'won't sit still' could justifiably be task avoidance if the task involves written work. Parents will often confirm that during the preschool years their child showed little inclination to draw, colour or pretend-write and so a downward spiral of potential failure had already begun (see Fig. 5.1). (For the development of handwriting refer to Chapter 4.4.)

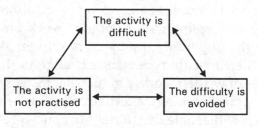

Figure 5.1 The downward spiral of potential failure

During the infant years handwriting takes the form of printing individual shapes so that a letter is a drawn picture and a word is a collection of these individual pictures. The dyspraxic child may, with great effort, learn to copy these pictures but the result is often larger and less uniform in size than for their classmates. Lines which define the space can help – a blank sheet of paper gives no visual cues to help organise the task. However, it is essential that the paper is specially prepared for the child so that the spaces match the current size of letters made by the child.

By the age of seven a transformation phase to a mature form of writing begins for most children. The hand writes a word image and the eye checks and reorganises the pattern if necessary. A mature adult is able to write for a short period of time with eyes open or eyes closed and produce an almost identical script because of proprioceptive feedback. A proprioceptive memory has become established for high-frequency words. The role of the eye is one of organisation and checking so that the eye checks the path taken, the letter formation and the limits of the writing space.

The dyspraxic child has to rely more heavily on visual monitoring when writing because s/he has less efficient proprioceptive feedback as well as poor fine-motor control. The results of this are:

- proprioceptive memories of the writing patterns are often difficult to establish and unreliable;
- a reduction in potential output because the eye is not only doing its normal job of organising and evaluating what is written but also having to check on hand movements;
- the writing is 'untidy' and 'messy' because of proprioceptive confusions about direction, non-standardised letter formation.

It is often necessary to teach writing patterns so that the child is able to do some independent work in the classroom. This is best done by practising letter combinations:

- use guide lines to define the physical space for writing;
- large scale: for maximum kinaesthetic feedback from hand and arm as well as fingers;
- large scale: for maximum feedback of left to right progression;
- on a vertical surface: so that 'up' and 'down' have meaning.

Once the patterns are established the size can be reduced, the skill can be transferred to a sloping surface (a flat table is not the best surface for writing) and the skills practised to fluency.

Some occupational therapists are, however, cautious about teaching handwriting as a splinter skill without work on sensory integration to solve the underlying problem. A splinter skill can easily break down as the curriculum demands change in the direction of greater quantities of written work, produced at faster speeds.

For many dyspraxic children, alternative means of recording can be devised which will enable the student to concentrate on the content of their written work and achieve some degree of independence when recording.

A visit to any mainstream classroom shows that children in any year group come in a range of sizes and shapes but this is seldom reflected in the classroom furniture. Most children are able to manage with less than optimal seating arrangements when writing. The dyspraxic child who will often experience trunk and or pelvic girdle instability, will find it more difficult to make compensations so that a poor seating position and poor posture will have a more obvious effect upon their ability to write.

A child who experiences difficulties with handwriting often also experiences problems with spelling. There are several possible reasons for this link which include a child concentrating on the mechanics of handwriting at the expense of monitoring the spelling patterns.

Box 5.2 *Some alternatives to handwriting*
- the teacher or classroom assistant acts as a scribe;
- the child uses a tape recorder or dictaphone and parents or school staff type or write what he wants to say;
- for older children, access to a word processor may be very important but younger children may not be ready to use a keyboard without supervision;
- the words which the child is able to recognise are written on cards, filed as in a 'Breakthrough to Literacy' folder. The child composes sentences by placing the words in order on a rack or on a long card using Blu-tack or velcro. Teacher, classroom assistant, parent-helper can make a written record of the child's work;
- the use of diagrams, charts, graphs, mind maps and other forms of visual representation;
- the use of a cartoon grid to record a story or activity – the child draws in the pictures in the right order;
- picture cards that form a sequence, with their corresponding sentences, match/order/record.

Box 5.3 *The ideal writing position*
- the furniture fits the child;
- there is a sloping surface on which to write;
- the bottom is at the back of the chair so thighs are supported;
- feet are on the ground;
- body and head upright;
- forearms supported on the table;
- correct pencil grip.

(See Chapter 4.4.)

For mature skilled writers the proprioceptive memory of familiar words or spelling patterns helps with the accurate spelling of words, so that the visual monitoring component is reduced. This proprioceptive memory may not develop in the same way for dyspraxic writers. When she learned to touch type, one girl said 'Now my fingers remember how the spellings go.'

Recording is not only about handwriting or finding a suitable alternative to handwriting, it is also about how what is recorded is set out on the page. Children with dyspraxia may experience particular difficulties with the spatial organisation which is the key to good presentation.

Children may find it hard to organise the setting out of their work, that is why their books 'look such a mess'. Helping to define the space available may make a noticeable difference to the child's presentation.

> **Box 5.4** *Strategies to help with the setting out of work*
> - coloured dots: green for the starting place, red for the finish, an orange dot to signal – don't start a new word after this sign;
> - the use of guide lines for writing;
> - a template for the setting out of the task prepared in advance, showing, for example, lines for where the heading and date go, a box in which to draw apparatus or a picture, guide lines for the writing;
> - the setting out of a maths task may be particularly difficult and column drift can make it harder to carry out mathematical processes accurately. Squared paper with the squares a suitable size for the child's writing skill can help, but some children may benefit from a template for each sum, numbered, on the page.

Visual perception and the dyspraxic child

The screening procedures in school will usually indicate that a dyspraxic child has no problems with vision. In the Chesson *et al.* study, twenty-three of the thirty-two children had been told that their vision was 'normal' following school checks and routine visits to the optician. The occupational therapy assessments subsequently revealed a rather different picture of the children's functional vision: Of the thirty-two children:

- twenty-three had problems with visual tracking;
- seventeen had problems with the rapid localisation of stimuli;
- other children experienced loss of the stimulus, mid-line avoidance, excessive head movements as an accompaniment to eye movements. Some children do experience ocular dyspraxia which is defined as an inability to move the eyes independently of the head.

At a life-skills level, visual perceptual problems can cause difficulty in recognising objects and their relationship to each other in space. The difficulty in making visual judgements may be highlighted in the area of ball skills for which the accurate assessment of the speed and direction of a moving projectile is a key to successful catching.

Visual perception and reading

For many children, difficulties with visual perception may only become apparent when the child starts to learn to read.

Case study 1

When J was nine, his mother commented in her contribution to his Statement of Educational Needs:

He does find the physical act of reading very difficult. His silent reading is better than his reading aloud but he has difficulty with sustained reading and often loses the meaning in a small print book. He was given glasses with the left eye occluded to help him develop a fixed reference eye and these have helped his attention span and concentration as long as he is reading a large print book. He may have exercises later to help improve his fixation on letters; due to his eye problems letters seem to swim.

J had made a promising initial start with reading when he was presented with single words or a limited number of words printed large on each page. His problems became apparent as the print size decreased, there were more words on the page and he was expected to read for longer periods of time. Typically children like J may frequently lose their place on the page and need to use a card to define each line for much longer than their classmates.

Box 5.5

Visual perceptual problems may affect progress with reading. The behavioural signs include:
- slow progress with reading in an otherwise able child;
- a reluctance to read more than a few lines;
- an unexpected reluctance to read when the child reaches a stage in the reading scheme where the print size is reduced;
- a reluctance to choose books with small print or many lines on a page;
- missing words or missing lines when reading aloud;
- looking up at regular intervals and fixating on distant objects. This may be misconstrued as a lack of attention;
- rubbing the eyes after reading for a variable length of time and/or head shaking or other 'tic'-like movements;
- screwing up one eye or occluding one eye;
- an asymmetrical posture when reading and writing;
- watering or red eyes after reading for a variable length of time.

A child should show more than half of the signs on a regular basis before there is cause for concern.

Visual perception and routine classroom activities

If the task is to copy from a board or a worksheet, there is an opportunity to struggle at phase 1 and 3 of the task:
1. locate place on board or worksheet;
2. retain the information;
3. locate place on page for writing;
4. return to 1 and continue 1 to 4 until the task is completed.

Copying from a board or wall chart may add in an extra dimension of difficulty as the child is required to translate a series of symbols

> **Box 5.6**   *Action plan*
> - advice from an ophthalmic consultant about dynamic, bin-ocular visual functioning (the movement of both eyes in a coordinated way);
> - access to enlarged texts or a Franklin magnifier (a sort of bar magnifier) according to the perceived need of the child;
> - some children find it easier to read text which is projected on to a vertical surface rather than presented at the normal reading distance;
> - shared reading of print of an appropriate font size to help to build up the required eye movement control, to practise decoding skills, to build up stamina for reading;
> - eye exercises, if these are recommended by the ophthalmologist.

presented in a vertical plane on to the horizontal surface of his paper.

When any difficulties that the child experiences with the mechanics of handwriting are added to the equation, it is not surprising that many dyspraxic children will attempt to avoid or rapidly abandon tasks which involve copy-writing even if it means incurring the wrath of their teacher.

Visual perceptual problems may affect areas of the curriculum other than through reading so that the matching or recognition of letters, numbers, symbols, words, shapes and the interpretation of pictures, diagrams, maps, graphs and charts may present problems for some children. These will be discussed in more detail with reference to the secondary curriculum.

The classroom as a working environment for the dyspraxic child
It will by now be apparent that many of the activities of the classroom which were defined by Professor Alexander (1992) as high-frequency will be difficult and unrewarding for a child with dyspraxia. The urge to escape, albeit temporarily, from a task may result in some wandering around the classroom, perhaps engaging in 'displacement activities' such as endless pencil sharpening. The wandering can, in itself, create difficulties with peers as well as the teacher. It can be distracting, intrusive and irritating to be interrupted frequently if you are trying to concentrate on a task and a dyspraxic child with a poor body image blunders into your table, trips over your bag or knocks things off the table as they go by.

A child who experiences planning difficulties will find it hard to organise the equipment which is required for a task and is, therefore, more likely to move around the classroom in search of items which are needed. Planning the execution of the task may present as many difficulties as the organisation of the materials which are needed.

Box 5.7 *Action plan*

Children who have a history of difficulties with motor control frequently find it hard to organise themselves and their equipment.

Task organisation

1. if instructions which involve a sequence of activities are given to the whole group, never assume that s/he will be able to carry out the task. Following the class instruction, with discretion, ask him/her to tell you what s/he is expected to do. The act of putting the task requirements into his/her own words and practising the recall of the sequence of the elements of the task will help him/her to structure the task;
2. once s/he becomes more confident s/he may be given the role of telling his/her work group what to do;
3. cue cards may help children to sequence a task, e.g.:
   a) clear your desk,
   b) collect the equipment that you need,
   c) put the date at the top of the page, etc.
   Some cue cards, like the example above, may apply to many tasks while others may be more specific, e.g. one which describes the steps of a mathematical process. If a child is unable to read a cue card, a pictorial representation of the sequence of activities may be a useful alternative.

Organisation of equipment

1. ensure that the equipment in the classroom is kept in the same place and that boxes, drawers, etc. are labelled clearly. Picture labels may be necessary for some children;
2. if it is hard for him/her to learn where things are kept, play a 'Fetch me . . .' game until s/he is able to find equipment with confidence;
3. the organisation of equipment may be difficult for some children. Cue cards may again be useful:
   a) the first instruction would be to 'clear your table of everything except for what you need',
   b) give the cue card (written or pictorial) which is specific to the task in hand, viz ruler, pencil, number book, ten unifix cubes,
   c) some teachers prepare a pack of cards, each of which has a picture of an item of equipment (e.g. ruler). The cards for each task are 'dealt' to the child,
   d) cue cards for the class might be displayed on a flip chart,
   e) a group of children who have organisation problems might work out what they require for a task using a pool of cue cards. The appropriate cards could then be displayed, e.g. on a magnetic board, on a hanging cue-card holder, etc.

Teachers are often uncomfortably aware that a child with motor problems seldom seems able to sit still or stand in line without leaning on someone or something. This behaviour often causes arguments among the children as the dyspraxic child is seen as invading the personal space of his classmates. This behaviour is often more apparent when the children are sitting close together on the carpet for story or circle time. A child with motor coordination problems and poor trunk stability will find it particularly hard to maintain balance when sitting unsupported on the floor. The difficulty can often be eased by seating the child in space, towards the edge of the group, on a chair. It may be that in the interest of fairness some way of ensuring that all children get the opportunity to sit on a bench or chair at times will need to be devised.

Practical group work might at first appear to offer some respite for the dyspraxic child, but the unskilled use of tools such as scissors, inaccurate pouring or measuring, a tendency to drop things, to knock things over and mislay vital bits of equipment can make them an unwelcome member of a work group.

The dyspraxic child in the classroom

Case study 2

T has a good general knowledge and vocabulary. At ten, his favourite TV programme is *Horizon* and he understands and remembers what he hears or sees. Assessments carried out by the educational psychologist showed that his abilities were well above average. However, his early verbal dyspraxia and phonological problems affect the intelligibility of his speech when he is excited, tired or anxious and contribute to his difficulties with reading and spelling. Although an optician would say that his vision is normal, he has difficulties with the control of his eye movements: convergence, pursuit and tracking, which make reading and copying difficult for T. He never reads for long periods.

T is able, at last, to write neatly albeit slowly but he can only sustain his effort for short periods of time. His short bursts of concentrated effort and his fatigue towards the end of the day or the week contribute to a variability in his performance that is hard for some of his teachers to accept.

T has difficulties with body control and balance so he appears to be restless and to fidget in his seat and not to stand still in line. He often trips over things and bumps into people as he moves around the classroom but most of his classmates have known him for years and are quite tolerant. T's mother is aware that he can get lost even in his familiar junior school and wonders how he will cope with moving around a big secondary school.

T's body awareness is poor but he can now dress himself without help, provided no one rushes him. He finds it hard to organise his possessions, his tasks and his equipment, so his teacher has been advised to use visual cue cards to help him with this. Year 5 has been quite difficult for T because some of the topics in maths, technology and science involve him using equipment in a coordinated way and T finds it hard to coordinate even tasks such as using a ruler to draw a line.

Perhaps because he is such an able boy, T finds it hard to accept how difficult it is for him to do some things which his classmates find easy. He has really good ideas but is unable to write them down, and often goes for the easy option of writing something short and predictable which only uses the simple words that he is able to spell. His teacher tries to give him opportunities to show his skills in class discussions and mental arithmetic sessions. Unfortunately, T's ideal-self is to be good at all the things his peers can do and value, such as reading, writing, completing classroom assignments and playing football. He tends to dismiss his areas of strength as unimportant and so his self-esteem remains low.

Peers and play in the primary years

Even before they start school, many dyspraxic children will have experienced difficulties interacting and playing with other children.
Parents say:

> 'I think the other children avoided him at playgroup because his speech was hard to understand.'

> 'When we went to the park he couldn't climb the steps to use the slide . . . he soon got tired and sat with me while his little sister ran round with the other children.'

In the first few weeks at school a child may be identified as the one who can't do things: steer the bike, climb on the apparatus, get undressed and dressed independently, draw, cut, stick, make Lego models. The image can be of someone who is unrewarding to play with or to be partnered with. In the early years at school play in the playground is predominantly active, physical play and children who can't join in effectively can become marginalised. Some children will react by ceasing to attempt to join in and thereby become isolated while some may vent their frustrations by showing aggressive behaviour.

However, aggressive behaviour among dyspraxic children may not, in fact, be as it seems. Children with a poor body image may bump into people or invade their body space by standing too close without any intention of being aggressive, although others may interpret their behaviour as a potential threat. Likewise a poor ability to control the force or direction of a movement may result in a friendly hand on the arm (intent) becoming to the receiver a blow to the chest to which the latter responds accordingly.

Someone in your group who always seems to knock things off the table, drop the model you have made, pours the water over you rather than into the measuring jar, can be seen as an irritant to be avoided and so the dyspraxic child is as often left out of work groups in the classroom as well as groups for PE.

PE and games

PE and games lessons are particularly stressful times for most dyspraxic children because in this context their movement difficulties are on open display. The skills of running, jumping, balancing, climbing, throwing and catching, all skills identified by the parents in the Chesson *et al.* study as problematical, are the core skills to which, for older children, are added the elements of team working and competition. Most dyspraxic children find ball skills particularly difficult because of the complexities of adapting the basic skills according to judgements about speed, direction and force of movement. Throwing the ball hard may be a skill but without some control over the direction of the throw it is of little use in a game. Some children try harder because of potential 'shaming' or are told to try harder but this sort of pressure often serves only to exaggerate the incorrect movements. Other children attempt to camouflage their lack of skill by clowning, e.g. 'pretending' to fall off the balance beam or 'falling over' when the exercise is to stop and maintain a balance. A common motto seems to be – I look like an idiot so I will play the idiot, the label of class clown is not so bad.

Early PE lessons may reveal difficulties with carrying out spatial directions such as under, over, forwards, backwards, behind, in front, next to and, of course, left and right. Learning sequences of movement such as the country dance routine for the May Day celebrations may also be a problem and the attendant behaviour be misunderstood. The teacher may say, 'He messed around all through the rehearsals but he could do it correctly on the day – that's what I mean about him being so naughty.'

PE and games lessons are times to be avoided for some children. Being always the last to get changed may reflect the reluctance to participate in the session as well as the practical difficulties of dressing and undressing in a defined period of time.

One boy, aged nine, complained of nausea and vomiting, but only on the days when they had PE. Observation during PE lessons can be very revealing when the teacher says the magic words of 'get into pairs or groups of . . .'.

Observation notes

For a moment R stood and watched the other children as they began to link up into small groups. As he approached the first group the two children just moved away and R drifted around again. He approached a second pair and they openly told him to go away. On this occasion the teacher acted as his partner but on other occasions he was put into a group with some sympathetic girls who were least likely to protest about having him on their team or in their group.

For action plans see the skill groups as described in Chapter 4.1.

The playground

When children are referred to the educational psychologist because of concerns about peer relationships, examples of playground behaviour are often quoted. A dyspraxic child may be described as a 'loner' and spend breaks with the adult on duty rather than making an attempt to join in with playground games which put a premium on many of the same skills as the PE or games lesson. In the playground there is usually no adult to manoeuvre a role for a dyspraxic child in an impromptu game.

Parents will often perceive playground problems as more significant than the problems which are experienced in the classroom. They describe experiences of bullying, ridicule and social isolation which have occurred in terms of a network of interrelated factors (see Fig. 5.2).

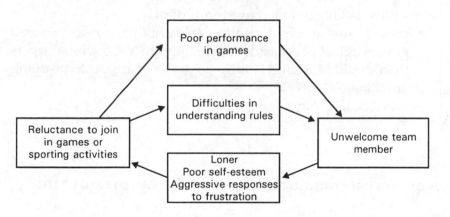

Figure 5.2   Interrelated factors of playground problems

Olveus (1978) in one of the earliest studies of bullying in schools found that 75 per cent of the victims of bullying had coordination problems. It is, therefore, important for all teachers to be aware that dyspraxic children and other clumsy students are at high risk for playground and classroom bullying.

At six years children play together using movements, physical actions, quick verbal exchanges and games with simple rules. The poorly coordinated child is seriously exposed. They stand out as being unable to respond appropriately and or quickly enough. They can become marginalised and excluded. By twelve years of age many children engage in little physical activity and during breaks they largely talk in groups. The poorly coordinated child does not stand out as they are simply one of many who are talking. There are significant implications for self-esteem here. Poor playground games playing is a major source of self-esteem problems for six and seven year olds while it is not for twelve year olds.

The same difficulties which make the playground an unfriendly place also tend to affect the children's experiences in out of school activities such as cubs, where competitive games and the ability to write are components of many of the core activities.

Dyspraxic children may experience more success in relationships with younger children who are less of a challenge to their competence or with older children and adults who are better able to accommodate to their needs.

Box 5.8 *Action plan*
- acknowledge that every school does have children for whom conventional playtime is stressful;
- provide an alternative option to going out for active, physical play such as a games/activity room where there are table top games, construction toys, etc.;
- provide the option of an adult-led game in the playground in which vulnerable children can be included;
- landscape the play area so that there are quiet areas for sitting, talking or less active forms of play;
- provide useful jobs for vulnerable children to do in small groups indoors or outside so that they are less obvious targets than would be a child alone who does not appear to be doing anything;
- social skills groups.

Non-verbal communication and the dyspraxic child

What teachers say:

'He is an unresponsive child, he just looks blank when I talk to him.'

'I never know if he has understood what I am telling him.'

'He never seems to get excited or enthusiastic about what we are doing.'

Some dyspraxic children appear to have particular difficulty with the organisation and control of the muscle groups which signal facial expression. They may, therefore, to those who do not understand, be 'deadpan' in facial expression, unresponsive or even defiant.

The importance of the ability to signal your feelings to others and to read the facial expressions of others was highlighted in two studies of preschool children. Spence (1987) and Walden and Field (1990) found that even at playgroup, children who were able to show their emotions in facial expressions and to respond appropriately to the non-verbal behaviour of the other children were more popular than the children who were less skilled in doing these things.

Box 5.9

Spence (1987) studied sixty children who were aged between three and five years. She found that the children who could tell what other children were feeling from the facial expression of their peers and act appropriately were chosen more often by other children. Walden and Field (1990) found that the ability to express feelings and the ability to interpret the expressions of others were related. Friendship choices among preschool children were predicted by:
- the ability to identify feelings from facial expression;
- the spontaneous ability to express feelings on one's face.

The perceived lack of responsiveness of some dyspraxic children may begin to affect their relationships with their peers even before the latter start to make value judgements about their competence in other areas of functioning.

Box 5.10 *Action plan*
- use a mirror to help children to copy facial expressions;
- teach the label for the emotion which goes with the expression, e.g. a 'sad face'. Pictures of familiar people showing different emotions can be useful for this, e.g. parents or teachers;
- practise in front of the mirror making faces which fit different verbal labels;
- practise in a group the signalling of different emotions in response to picture stimuli, verbal instructions or life events;
- practise in a group the interpretation of the facial expressions of others;
- generalise the skills into the home and the classroom.

The awkward gait and unusual, stooped posture of many children with motor coordination problems can also affect how others perceive them. In nature a stooped posture is submissive and may almost 'invite' bullying at an instinctive level in some people. Lorraine Burr of Northwick Park Hospital has written about how occupational therapy can result in improved posture which in turn may have a positive effect upon relationships. A headteacher commented 'When he comes into my room now he looks at me and I feel that I can talk to him.' This child was also reported to have begun to make friends.

Psychosomatic symptoms

It is a rare child who does not occasionally complain of a tummy ache on some school mornings because they do not want to face the day. For a child with movement problems normal, everyday activities will take longer and require more effort from them and so they are inevitably going to feel more tired at the end of the day or the week than their classmates. However, for some children the routine social and academic expectations in the school environment can result in high levels of stress and anxiety. One common sign of high levels of stress may be complaints of non-organic pain such as headaches, stomach aches or feelings of nausea. These may be worse after a weekend or holiday or even have a higher incidence on some days of the week, e.g. Friday – spelling test, or Wednesday – PE. There may be more specific reactions of the type that psychiatrists would call 'hysterical conversions' such as complaining of leg pains because of anxieties about PE and games. Unless these early signs of stress are recognised and appropriate action taken to relieve the stress, there is always the danger that a child might become a school refuser.

The secondary school

For a dyspraxic child, the secondary school environment presents new challenges in the form of:

- the demands of the curriculum;
- the organisation of timetables and homework;
- social relationships and self-esteem.

The transfer to secondary school can be difficult for many children and their families may be aware of changes in their behaviour. Some dyspraxic children may show quite dramatic stress-related reactions at this time.

J's mother said:

> 'He often acts in a babyish way, using immature language, demanding cuddles, hitting his sister. When he feels he has had a bad day at school his frustration can lead him to bang his head on the wall – often the triggers for these outbursts can seem very trivial.'

Fortunately, J's mother was able to share her concerns with the SENCO at his secondary school and he was given more curriculum support and help with the organisational aspects of secondary school life. The level of stress which J had been experiencing had only shown itself at home and so it was very important that his mother was able to liaise with the SENCO.

The curriculum

Secondary school provides the opportunity for children to develop skills in a range of subjects, some of which may give experiences of success that serve to boost self-esteem. By Year 9 J was proud of his progress in maths and science. Other subject areas may serve to exacerbate the difficulties with recording or reading which s/he experienced at primary school because more is expected in terms of both the quantity and quality of written work. Although most secondary school teachers will decry the practices of dictating to the class or writing on the board for the children to copy, most students will refer to difficulties keeping up with note-taking or copying from the board. Homework may be a significant new issue. Some of the strategies which were used at primary school to support reading and recording, e.g. the classroom assistant acting as a scribe, may no longer be socially acceptable to the child at secondary school. The focus at the secondary phase should be on the development of independence as a learner and so some of the strategies used at primary school should be phased out if they do not meet this criterion.

Box 5.11   *Action plan*
Strategies for recording:
- lesson notes taken by the classroom assistant or summary notes prepared in advance by the teacher;
- access to word processing facilities and a printer. Students who have not received touch-typing lessons at primary school may benefit from a 'typing tutor' programme in Year 7 to ensure that their typing is up to speed;
- the use of a dictaphone for drafts of project work, preparation of ideas for written assignments, etc.;
- the use of mind-maps as an alternative way of taking notes or drawing diagrams of the main ideas in a text;
- the provision of the outlines of diagrams, apparatus drawings, maps, etc. so that the student only has to label the relevant parts or annotate the diagrams;
- parents may have the dedication to act as scribe in the privacy of the home and thereby take some of the pressure off homework tasks.

Box 5.12   *Alternatives to reading*
- the use of audio tapes of set books that may be commercially available;
- recording of written texts by support staff or parents;
- the presentation of written material in the form of diagrams, mind-maps, for those students who are able to interpret this type of information.

Some subjects at secondary school may make demands of a different order and complexity which a dyspraxic student will find it hard to meet. For example, technology may involve the carefully co-ordinated use of instruments for technical drawing or the safe use of tools such as saws or drills. Some severely affected students may need support during science practicals or in food technology where they may be required to handle potentially dangerous chemicals or equipment. It is not always easy for a school to plan the flexibility into the support package which will enable an assistant to be present in some sessions according to the specific tasks which are planned. The priority sessions for support will need to be considered according to the developmental profile of each student and individually planned. The students themselves will often have quite clear ideas about the lessons in which they need support and will express their personal preferences about in-class vs withdrawal as a means of delivery. J was quite clear that he wanted help at secondary school because he 'wanted to show people that he wasn't dim'.

In Year 9 there is the ideal opportunity to review with a student their progress in all areas of the curriculum and to plan a sensible choice of options for Year 10 and Year 11 which will accommodate their strengths and not overload them in terms of written assignments in particular. Some students may take a reduced number of GCSE options and add a study skills option so that they can spend more time on the subjects they do take.

It is possible for special arrangements to be made for dyspraxic candidates in GCSE examinations. Schools may apply for special arrangements for course work as well as for unseen examinations. The request for special arrangements would normally be accompanied by a report from the educational psychologist based on assessments carried out within eighteen months of the date of the examinations. An assessment carried out early in Year 10 could be used to support a request for concessions for any modular exams as well as remaining valid, with minimal updating, for the Year 11 examinations. The senior member of staff who is responsible for examination arrangements will know which examination board is involved for each subject that the student is taking. Although all examining groups make some special provision for candidates according to need, there are differences in the percentage of the final grade which is derived from course work and the type of concessions which are allowed.

Exam concessions

The factors which the examining boards will take into account and are relevant to dyspraxic candidates include:
- speed of writing;
- speed of reading;
- fatigue effects which may reduce performance over time;
- the number of subjects taken and the timetable for the exams;
- the requirement for drawing diagrams which may result in extra time being needed;
- extra time needed to carry out practical tasks.

A range of options is available which may include:
- 25 per cent extra time to complete the question paper;
- rest periods with fifteen minutes in the hour added to the time to accommodate these;
- the use of a word processor (with the more sophisticated functions, e.g. spellcheck, suppressed);

- a reader under tightly specified conditions;
- an amanuensis;
- tape recording;
- presentation of a transcript if the student's writing is difficult to read. Together with additional time, this may be a preferred option;
- special arrangements for the oral components of an exam if speech is unintelligible.

Personal organisation

The regime of the secondary school imposes demands for personal organisation which are very different from those of the primary school, however well the children have been prepared.

Particular challenges for the dyspraxic student may include:

- *learning their way around the new building:* they often have no close friends to go around with, are more likely to get lost and less likely to have strategies for finding where they should be. Extra trips to the school when there are few children about so that they can practise navigation skills, e.g. from science lab to canteen, carrying a map and having an emergency plan may all be reassuring;
- *carrying all their equipment for the day or part of the day around with them:* as all motor movements require more effort, stamina and fatigue become significant. Also losing or leaving behind bags, books or equipment is a frequent occurrence, so naming items can help;
- *organising the books and equipment they will need for the day or part of the day and ensuring that the things are in their bag:* parents can play a key support role in ensuring that the student starts off with the correct equipment. Bags with compartments so that most-used items such as pens are easily accessible can be helpful. If everything has to be tipped out at the start of a lesson, there is more chance of losing things and the time taken to repack the bag may distract other children and irritate the teacher. When most things are taken out of the bag it may be hard for the student to repack them at the end of the lesson;
- *adapting the style of the presentation of work to the requirements of the subject and the preferences of the teacher:* a dyspraxic student may have worked out an acceptable strategy for organising tasks and setting out their work at primary school but this may not be flexible to new demands. Subject teachers will need to be aware of their difficulties and coloured stickers on the class list can alert the subject teachers to special needs. Different coloured stickers can signal different needs, e.g. medical, reading problems, writing problems;
- *coping with a canteen at lunchtime:* a dyspraxic student may find it hard to balance a tray, hang on to the school bag and at the same

time attempt to get money out to pay for lunch. If eating is still a messy process other children may avoid sitting near the dyspraxic student.

Homework

J's mother said in Year 7:

> 'He does get very tired and his coordination, speech and behaviour are noticeably less controlled at the end of the day.'

> 'He is very tired by the evening and finds any extended task very frustrating.'

> 'He does his homework after tea and tries to do it without my writing it out for him as children have teased him that it is "cheating" to have secretarial assistance.'

In an effort to be conscientious and keep up with classmates, the dyspraxic student may spend a disproportionately long time doing homework and stay up late in order to complete assignments. They may feel they need to do several drafts and a neat copy and this is exacerbated if teachers criticise presentation. The result can be a downward spiral of fatigue and stress. Other dyspraxic students may adopt the opposite strategy of denying that they have homework – ever.

Complications can arise when the student and his parents have difficulty interpreting what is written in the homework diary. Teachers do still give instructions about homework at the end of a lesson when the children are trying to jot it down quickly, while packing their bags so they will not be late for the next lesson.

It is important for parents to help the school to be aware of difficulties with homework as special arrangements can often be made which may include:

- differentiation of homework tasks if necessary;
- a clear message that alternatives to handwriting such as use of the word processor, a scribe or a tape are acceptable for some students;
- time to use the word processor and printer in school if these are not available at home;
- requests to subject teachers or classroom assistants to write the homework in the homework diary;
- time in support studies to help with homework assignments that the student has found difficult;
- support in advance to organise topic work or projects which will extend over several homeworks;
- a clear message that the homework should only take __ minutes and that it is acceptable not to finish if parents sign the work to say that the student did try for that amount of time;

- a homework club after school when any students can receive support for assignments that they find difficult.

The complexities of the timetable may mean that homeworks are set on one day to be done on a different evening to be handed in on yet another day. It is a difficult feat of organisation to remember what needs to be done when. The homework timetable displayed prominently may help with one aspect of the problem. It may also be useful to have a set of organiser trays labelled with the days of the week into which books and equipment needed for specific days can be put so that they can be packed into the bag before the student goes to bed or first thing in the morning.

Social relationships and self-esteem

The pattern of uneasy social relationships with peers that was evident even before school and consolidated at the primary phase is unlikely to improve in secondary school without specific intervention. A few fortunate children may have been involved in social skills training groups during their primary phase and be better placed to establish new relationships when they start at secondary school. Some secondary schools do have social skills training groups for Year 7 students which may be appropriate for the dyspraxic student.

J's mother said:

> 'One longs for him to have a friend to potter about with in the holidays.'

> 'He finds social interaction with his peers very difficult.'

Expressions of low personal esteem (J – 'I'm rubbish') reflect both a lack of a sense of achievement in terms of key areas of the curriculum and a failure to establish and maintain any lasting friendships.

> J 'becomes ashamed of and upset about his work when he realises what others have achieved . . . we have tried our best to give him a sense of self-worth'.

It is important for parents and teachers to acknowledge what the dyspraxic student does do well and to reward progress in the areas which they find more difficult. It is unfortunate that some children with low self-esteem like T (case study 2) will dismiss the things that they can do well (debate and discuss ideas) as being of little importance unless everyone is able to give a clear, consistent message that they are *good* at this and it is a *valued* skill. It may sometimes be helpful to introduce a child to an activity at which they may be successful. For example, many dyspraxic people can swim quite well once they have coordinated the stroke patterns. They are much more likely to get pleasure from swimming and compete on equal terms with their peers than in any sport which involves a ball. Some PE departments in secondary schools can be quite sympathetic and imaginative so that they adapt the range of games options to provide some more rewarding, or at least less embarrassing, alternative activities for the students who have movement difficulties. Some students may be given the option of taking support studies during games lessons provided that their parents are willing to ensure that they get some suitable exercise such as swimming each week. Students who have had the opportunity to attend motor skills groups (see Chapter 4.1) at primary school will be better prepared to join in with the physical curriculum at secondary school. To no longer be the worst at every activity and sometimes to be picked for a team rather than be left until last can have a very positive effect upon self-esteem.

The positive regard of others is the other cornerstone on which self-esteem is built. In Year 9 J was still finding relationships difficult:

> 'He finds break-time at school very difficult to cope with and says no one speaks to him except to tease him. To fill his break-times he has become a fervent reader of the careers guide in the classroom . . .'

> 'He does not have friends in class and says he sometimes hears sniggers about himself when groups are being formed.'

However, J had joined three clubs at school, orienteering, maths club and young engineers, and he was finding it easier to be accepted in these groups where the participants shared a mutual interest and he had areas of skill which were valued by the group.

The self-concept and self-esteem

The self-concept is the sum of an individual's mental and physical characteristics and how that person evaluates these characteristics. It has three components:

Self-image
Self-image begins to build up as a consequence of our interactions with other people. From our first interactions with parents we begin to experience other people's perceptions of us as, for example, loveable/not loveable, clever/stupid. As children grow older, they pick up the messages (verbal and non-verbal) from extended family members, from adults in the community, from peers and from teachers. Cooley (1962) said that we form our self-image from the feedback we receive from 'significant others'. This was known as the looking glass theory of self.

Ideal self

Everyone forms ideas about the personal qualities which are admired and valued by significant people in their lives. We compose a picture of what we would like to be and for a dyspraxic child an ability to write quickly and neatly or to score a goal may be key components of their ideal self.

We go on adjusting our self-image and ideal self throughout life but the main formative years are birth to late teenage. Adults will clearly be the most 'significant others' during the early years with peers becoming more important as a child becomes less dependent upon adults for approval.

Self-esteem

We all compare our current self-image with our ideal self and the gap which we perceive exists between the two forms our self-esteem. The wider the gap the lower our self-esteem. Failure in itself does not result in low self-esteem, it is the way that significant others view that failure which affects self-esteem. Six and seven year olds are particularly vulnerable to developing self-esteem difficulties. Not only is the dyspraxic child at risk of failing in the playground but also in the classroom where they can be having real difficulties with handwriting. They are often by this stage one of a few children who can't write yet or can't write properly. In many areas of development seven is the age at which self-esteem problems can become more significant than the child's underlying difficulties would necessarily predict, because of the attitudes expressed towards them by significant others – peers, teacher and parents. It is very important that strategies to build self-esteem are also put in place early in the life of a child as it is very difficult to alter self-esteem because people tend to look for, and therefore to find, information which confirms their poor view of themselves. This tendency to look for information which is consistent with our self-image and accepting it is called *biased scanning*.

Parents and teachers are significant others and can have a powerful influence on the development of a child's self-image if they work together consistently to help to build a positive self-image.

Strategies which may help build self-esteem:

- set tasks which have a 'real' physical challenge, not a 'lets-pretend-it's-difficult' challenge. Overcome the challenge by directly supporting the child physically, i.e. two adult helpers to assist when crossing a bar, and letting the child decide when to lessen the support;
- reward all successes with real congratulations and praise;
- make all goals attainable;
- by observation, decide what it is a child can't do and, by task analysis, teach the elements;
- set clear, simple rules for engagement – 'tell me *one* thing you have done since . . .';
- have 'feedback' sessions at the end of every lesson to include an element of success for everyone;

- keep a supply of sweets handy to reward success;
- ensure that child and staff are aware of and acknowledge good points of character, e.g. kindness, generosity, willingness to continue trying, etc.;
- convey by your own manner that the child can achieve the goal.

Throughout this book we have stressed the importance of early identification and intervention if children experience problems with motor development. Strategies can be put in place which are designed both to improve basic skills and to minimise the impact of the problems at home and at school. Unacknowledged problems can continue to affect an individual throughout life.

Appendix

Points for identification

Poor shape perception.
Poor visual spatial skills.
Poor scanning – jerky eye movements, change of eye at mid-line.

Excessive movement, cannot sit still.
Inability to maintain body stillness.
Poor ability to queue – always last.
Pushes into things.
Knocks into furniture/other children.
Knocks over paint. Messy drawing/or other things in drawing.
Inability to move body spatially in relation to other people or objects.
Poor body awareness.
Poor directional skills.

PE:
- lost belongings;
- very slow to dress/undress;
- shoes on wrong feet;
- carries out wrong instruction;
- either stands still or races around/fools around (when class performing activity).

Compensatory movements.
Movement 'overshoots'.
Jerky movements.
Inability to carry out sequence of movement.
Makes the 'wrong movement' before correction.
Increased/decreased muscle tone.
Poor fluency and rhythm in movement.
Inability to change direction without overbalancing.
Inability to cross the mid-line.
Changes dominance.
Inability to estimate speed, direction, distance and/or time.

Observation guidelines for motor organisational problems

Poor mixing with peers, few or no friends.
Blamed for hitting.
Unresponsive in facial expression and/or body language
Seldom chosen as a partner for games and activities

Poor scissor skills.
Poor individual finger skills.
Overlap of movement into opposing limb.
Poor unilateral hand skills.
Continuous mobility of the small muscles of the hand.
Absence of a refined pincer grasp.
During oppositions fingers remain extended.
Poor design copying.

Difficulty in listening/following instructions.
Never learns instructions given to class.
Follows others in group.
Slow to express himself verbally.
Forgets instruction when asked to fetch something, especially if more than one article.
Word-finding problems.
Slow response to commands.
Does not name right or left.

Food all over face.
Difficulty using knife and fork.
Slow eater or doesn't chew, puts all in his mouth.

Attention seeking in classroom, e.g. class clown.
Poor divided attention.
Needs encouragement to complete tasks.
Does not complete tasks.
Immaturity.

Poor sense of time, always late.
No idea what time of day.
Unable to read clock beyond age of peers.

Glossary

Movement	Actual observable change in position of any part of the body. The culminating act of underlying motor processes and perception.
Movement pattern	An organised series of related movements.
Reflexes	An involuntary action caused by the stimulation of a sensory nerve ending or receptor.
Voluntary movements	A planned action or series of actions. A voluntary movement is initiated in the brain and a message is passed through motor nerves to the muscles.
Movement skill	A pattern with accuracy, precision and control.
Motor organisation	The putting together in the correct combination and order all the parts needed to be combined to produce a movement. The ability to plan and to execute a series of purposeful movements.
Gross-motor movement	Movements of the large muscles of the body: running, walking, kicking, catching, striking.
Fine-motor movement	Movements of the small muscles. Manipulative: sewing, handwriting, talking, eye movements and movements needed in all instances of accuracy, precision and control.
Acquired apraxia	A motor skill lost by an adult because of accident, age, infirmity or disease.
Developmental dyspraxia	A neurologically based difficulty that becomes evident as a baby develops.

Action errors	Force, timing, amplitude of movement.
Spatial awareness	Firstly, knowledge of the space occupied by the body and the position of bits of the body in space. Includes reference to the position of nearby objects. Secondly, the ability to project body or bits of the body into new space.
Directional awareness	Up-down, front-back, side-side. Laterality: internal feel for dimensions of the body. Directionality: projection of laterality to objects in space.

Useful addresses

AFASIC (Association for All Speech Impaired Children)
347 Central Markets, Smithfield, London EC1A 9NH.
Tel: 0171 236 3632

British Dyslexia Association
98 London Road, Reading, Berkshire.
Tel: 01734 662677

The Dyslexia Trust
133 Gresham Road, Staines, Middlesex TW18 3BA.
Tel: 01784 463851

The College of Speech and Language Therapists
7 Bath Place, Rivington Street, London EC2A 3DR.
Tel: 0171 613 3855

I CAN (Invalid Children's Aid Nationwide)
10 Bowling Green Lane, London EC1R 0BD.
Tel: 0171 253 9111

Dyspraxia Foundation
8 West Alley, Hitchin, Hertfordshire SG5 1EG
Tel: 01462 455016. Fax 01462 455052 Helpline 01462 454986

Chartered Society of Physiotherapy
14 Bedford Way, London WC1R 4ED.
Tel: 0171 306 6666

The British Association of Occupational Therapists
6/8 Marshalsea Road, Southwark, London SE1 1HL.

References

Alexander, R. (1992) *Policy and practice in primary education*. London: Routledge.

Ayres, A. J. (1972) *Sensory integration and learning disorders*. Los Angeles: Western Psychological Services.

Baker, L. and Cantwell, D. P. (1987) 'A prospective psychiatric follow-up of children with speech/language disorders', *Journal of the American Academy of Child Psychiatry* **26**, pp. 546–53.

Beery, K. E. (1989) *Developmental test of visual motor integration*. Cleveland, OH: Modern Curriculum Press.

Brindley, C., Cave, D., Crane, S., Lees, J. and Moffat, V. (1996) *POSP* (Paediatric Oral Skills Package). London: Whurr Publishers.

Cermak, S. A. (1985) 'Developmental dyspraxia', in E. A. Roy (ed.) *Neuropsychological studies of apraxia and related disorders*. Amsterdam: North Holland, pp. 225–48.

Chesson, R., McKay, C. and Stephenson, E. (1991) 'The consequences of motor/learning difficulties for *Learning* 6(4).

Conrad, K., Cermak, S. A. and Drake, C. (1983) 'Differentiation of praxis among children', *American Journal of Occupational Therapy* **37**, pp. 466–73.

Conti-Ramsden, G. (1987) *Mother–child talk with language-impaired children*. Proceedings of First International Symposium Specific Speech and Language Disorders in Children, University of Reading. London: AFASIC.

Cooley, C. 1962. *Human nature and the social order*. New York: Charles Scribner.

Crary, M. A. (1984) 'A neurolinguistic perspective on developmental dyspraxia', *Communicative Disorders* **IX**(3), pp. 33–49.

Curry, D. (1991) 'Breaking the cycle of failure', *Special Children*, June/July.

Dawdy, S. C. (1981) 'Paediatric neuropsychology: caring for the developmentally dyspraxic child', *Clinical Neuropsychology* **8**, pp. 367–79.

Dean, E. and Howell, J. (1986) 'Developing linguistic awareness: a theoretically based approach to phonological disorders', *British Journal of Disorders of Communication* **21**(2), pp. 223–38.

Dewey, D. and Kaplan, B. J. (1992) 'Analysis of praxis task demands in the assessment of children with developmental motor difficulties', *Developmental neuropsychology* **8**, pp. 367–79.

Dunn, M. L. (1979) *Skill starters for motor development*. Tucson, AZ: Communication Skill builders Inc.

Dutton, K. (1989) *Writing under examination conditions*. Glasgow: Scottish Education Department Regional Psychological Service.

Edwards, M. (1984) *Disorders of Articulation*. New York: Springer-Verlag.

Gallahue, D. (1982) *Understanding Motor Development in Children*. London: Wiley.

Henderson, S. E. and Hall, D. (1982) 'Concomitants of clumsiness in young school children', *Developmental Medicine and Child Neurology* **24**, pp. 448–60.

Henderson, S. E. and Sugden, D. A. (1992) *Movement assessment battery for children*. Sidcup, Kent: The Psychological Corporation.

Howell, J. and Dean, E. (1987) ' "I think that's a noisy sound": reflection and learning in the therapeutic situation', *Child Language, Teaching and Therapy* **3**(3), pp. 259–66.

Klick, S. L. (1985) 'Adapted cuing technique for use in the treatment of dyspraxia', *Language, Speech and Hearing Services in Schools* **6**(4), pp. 256–60.

Lord, R. and Hulme, C. (1988) 'Visual perception and drawing ability in normal and clumsy children', *British Journal of Developmental Psychology* **6**, 1–9.

Luria, A. R. (1980) *Higher cortical functions in management*. New York: Basic Books.

Miller, N. (1986) *Dyspraxia and its management*. London: Croom Helm.

Milloy, N. R. (1991) *Breakdown of speech, causes and remediation*. London: Chapman and Hall.

Morley, M. (1965) *The development of disorders of speech in childhood* (2nd edn). London: Churchill Livingstone.

Nuffield Dyspraxia Programme (1985). London: The Nuffield Hearing and Speech Centre.

Olveus, D. (1978) *Aggression in the schools: bullies and whipping-boys*. London: Wiley, Halstead Press.

Orton, S. J. (1937) *Reading, writing and speech problems in children*. New York: Norton.

Passey, J. (1985) *Cued articulation and cued vowels*. Northumberland: STASS Publications.

Pembrey, M. (1992) 'Genetics and language disorder', in P. Fletcher and D. Hall (eds) *Specific speech and language disorders in children*. London: Whurr Publishers.

Roy, E. A., Elliot, D., Dewey, D. and Square-Storar, P. (1991) 'Impairments to praxis and sequencing in adult and developmental disorders', in C. Bard, M. Fleury and L. Hay (eds) *Development of eye-hand co-ordination across the life span*. Columbia, SC.: University of South Carolina Press, pp. 358–84.

Sassoon, R. and Briem, J. (1993) *Teach yourself better handwriting*. London: Hodder Headline.

Spence, S. (1987) 'The relationship between social-cognitive skills and peer sociometric status', *British Journal of Developmental Psychology* **5**, pp. 347–56.

Walden, T. A. and Field, T. M. (1990) 'Pre-school children's social competence and production and discrimination of affective expressions', *British Journal of Developmental Psychology* **8**, pp. 65–76.

Walker, M. (1980) *The revised Makaton vocabulary*. St George's Hospital, London. Published by the author.

Wendon, L. (1986) *Letterland I and II* (revised). Cambridge: Letterland.

Index

Alexander, R., *Policy and Practice in Primary Education* 36, 69, 74
assessment of dyspraxic children 9, 10, 16–20, 58, 69, 72
Ayres, A. J., *Sensory Integration and Learning Disorders* 4–5

Baker, L and Cantwell, D. P., *A Prospective Psychiatric Follow-up of Children with Speech/Language Disorders* 66
balance 5, 9, 23, 26, 78
ball skills 9, 30–31, 67, 72, 78
Beery, K. E., *Developmental Test of Visual Motor Integration* 20
behaviour *see* socially unacceptable behaviour
body 3, 6, 19, 22–8, 66
brain 3, 8–9, 10, 23, 26
bullying 79, 81
Burr, L. 81

carers *see* parents
case studies of dyspraxic children 48, 52, 72–3, 76–7
Cermak, S. A., *Developmental Dyspraxia* 5, 65
Chesson, R. et al., *The Consequences of Motor/learning Difficulties for School-age Children and their Teachers: Some Parental Views* 21, 65, 67, 68, 72, 78
Child Development Centres 48
children
  images of dyspraxic children 17
  relationships with dyspraxic children 77–8, 79–80, 81

climbing 9, 25, 29, 78
Code of Practice 15–16, 20
cognitive abilities, assessment of 20, 21
communication 65–6, 80
competition 29, 79
confidence 6, 25, 29
Conrad, K. et al., *Differentiation of Praxis among Children* 5
Conti-Ramsden, G., *Mother-child Talk with Language-impaired Children* 54
conversation 54
Cooley, C. H., *Human Nature and the Social Order* 88
coordination *see* motor control
Crary, M. A., *A Neurolinguistic Perspective on Developmental Dyspraxia* 43
cuing 51

dance 28–9, 78
Dawdy, S. C., *Paediatric Neuropsychology: Caring for the Developmentally Dyspraxic Child* 1
development
  neurological 34–5
  rates of progress 10, 24
developmental approach to dyspraxia 8, 9, 10, 19
developmental education 8–9, 10–11
Dewey, D. and Kaplan, B. J., *Analysis of Praxis Task Demands in the Assessment of Children with Developmental Motor Difficulties* 5
disease, neurological 1

doctors   13, 14, 15, 23
drama   54
drawing   41–2
dressing   9, 33–4, 66, 78
dribbling   45, 47, 48
Dutton, K., *Writing under Examination Conditions*   41
dyspraxia   1, 13, 19, 64
  developmental   1–3, 93
    difficulties caused by   4–5
  ideational (planning)   5, 19, 66, 74–5
  ideo-motor (execution)   5
  ocular   72
  oral   45, 56–63
  verbal   17, 43–56
    language work   52–4, 55
    preschool   47–8
    and social skills   54
dyspraxic children
  attitudes to   64
  case studies   48, 52, 72–3, 76–7
  in the classroom   74–8, 82–4
  needs   11, 20, 24
  relationships with peers   79–80
  self-image   6, 7, 19, 77, 88–9
  ways of dealing with   54–5

eating   56–63
education
  developmental   8–9, 10–11
  secondary   82–4
Education Act (1993)   15
educational psychologists *see* psychologists
Edwards, M., *Disorders of Articulation*   43
environment, and development of movement   3, 8–9
epilepsy   19
examinations, special arrangements   83–4
exercise   29
eyes   23, 70, 74

facial expression   17, 23, 80–81
fault finding, as investigative approach   8, 11
feeding   16–17, 44–5, 56–63, 67
finger strength   24, 31, 42
fitness   29

Gallahue, D, *Understanding Motor Development in Children*   3

games
  for special educational groups   28
  see also physical education; play; skills
generalisation of skills   4, 8, 81
goals
  developmental   8–9, 11–12, 14, 19, 33
    and step-by-step teaching   24
  personal   25–6, 27
groups, special educational   25–6, 27, 28, 49, 88

hand dominance   36–7
handwriting   6, 10, 23, 26, 34–42, 68
  aids   24, 38, 70, 71
  alternatives to   11, 70, 71, 83, 86
  development   36–42, 69–70
  grip   37–8
  and hand dominance   36–7
  importance in schools   36, 69, 82–3
  learning basic patterns   38–9
  and motivation   34
  and numbers   35
  paper for   40
  and spatial ability   71–2
  strategies for progress   35–6, 70
  support activities   42
  tools for   40, 41
health visitors   13, 14
Henderson, S. E. and Sugden, D. A., *Movement Assessment Battery for Children*   1, 20
homework   83, 86–7

identification   13–15, 21, 90–92
independence, as educational goal   19, 83
Individual Education Plans   15

jumping   25, 29, 67, 78

language   46, 52–4, 55–6, 66
language therapists *see* speech therapists
Language Units   49
left handers   31, 37
Letterland   51
Luria, A. R.   3

Makaton signing system   48, 51
manipulation *see* skills
Metaphon   50

Miller, N., *Dyspraxia and its Management* 1
Milloy, N. R., *Breakdown of Speech, Causes and Remediation* 45
motor control 23, 29, 34, 56–7, 64
  coordination 3, 4, 6, 8, 10, 23
  fine-motor control 6, 31, 69–70
  see also muscle control
movements
  apparently involuntary 23–4
  associated 26
  involuntary 19
  oral, control of 45, 56–8
  vocabulary for 28
  voluntary 1
    development of 3–4, 8–9, 22–3, 24, 29–30
muscle control 4, 17, 25, 45–6
  see also motor control
music 28, 51, 52, 53–4

National Curriculum 20
nose-blowing 46, 61–2
Nuffield Dyspraxia Programme 50
numbers, and handwriting 35

occupational therapists 14, 21, 25, 34, 49, 70
  and assessment of dyspraxic children 18–19
occupational therapy 2, 48, 81
Olweus, D., *Aggression in the Schools: Bullies and Whipping-boys* 79
oral *see* movements; sensitivity; skills
Orton, S. J., *Reading, Writing and Speech Problems in Children* 64

paediatricians 14, 19
parents
  attitudes to dyspraxic children 54, 59, 66, 67–8
  images of dyspraxic children 6, 14, 17, 44
  and recognition of problem 13, 65–6, 67
  working with teachers 9, 15, 82
  working with therapists 19, 47
peers *see* children
perception, visual 50, 72–4
physical education (PE) 25, 53, 78, 82, 87–8
physiotherapists 25

physiotherapy 48
play 3, 14, 25, 29, 30
  difficulties with 12, 18, 77, 79–80
  with food 59, 60
  and stages of development 32–3
pouring 31, 76
praxis 1, 3, 5–6
proprioceptive system 4–5, 19, 50, 70, 71
psychologists
  educational 14, 15, 49
    and assessment of dyspraxic children 19–20, 21, 68

reading 51, 53, 68, 72–3, 83
Rebus manual signing system 51
referral 14, 15
reflexes 1, 19, 56
reporting on dyspraxic children, framework for 20–21
running 25, 29, 67, 78

safety 26, 31
Sassoon, R. and Briem, G. S. E., *Teach Yourself Better Handwriting* 38
school
  difficulties coping with 6–7, 14, 18, 25, 68-9, 73–4
    psychosomatic symptoms 68, 78, 81–2
  organisation for 75, 85–6
  secondary 82–4
  see also Code of Practice; groups; homework; physical education; teachers
schools, working with therapists 18, 49
scissors 31–2, 76
self-care
  difficulties coping with 14, 18
  see also dressing; nose-blowing
self-esteem 9, 18, 21
  and adolescence 25–6
  adversely affected 6, 18, 33, 67, 77, 79
  affected by identification 13
  building 89–90
  as educational goal 11, 19
  effects of 12
  promotion of 11, 19, 25, 35, 82
  and social relationships 87–8
  and swimming 29, 87–8
self-image 88–9

SENCO *see* Special Needs
 Coordinator
sensitivity, oral 58–60
Signed English signing system 51
signing 47, 48, 51
skills
  ball skills 9, 30–31, 67, 72, 78
  development through
   practice 11, 23–4
  generalisation of 4, 8, 81
  manipulative 30, 31–2
  oral 56–8, 60–61
  social 54, 87
  sports 25, 26, 29
  on wheels 30, 31, 67
social activities, difficulties with
 25, 77, 79, 87
socially unacceptable behaviour
 46, 65, 68, 76, 77
  feeding 44, 67
spatial ability 31, 71–2
spatial awareness 5, 6
special educational needs 20, 21,
 49
Special Needs Coordinator
 (SENCO) 15, 82
speech 6, 23, 43–6, 46, 53–4
speech and language therapists
 see speech therapists
speech organs 44, 45
speech therapists 14, 15, 47–8, 50
  and assessment of dyspraxic
   children 16–17, 23
  working with schools 18, 49
speech therapy 2, 50
spelling 70–71
Spence, S., *The Relationship between*

*Social/cognitive Skills and Peer
 Sociometric Status* 80–81
Statements of Special Educational
 Needs 15, 52, 72
support teachers 15
swimming 29, 87–8

tactile receptors 4, 19, 50
targets 25, 27
teachers
  images of dyspraxic children 6,
   7, 17
  misinterpretation of dyspraxic
   behaviour 25, 68–9
  understanding of dyspraxia
   9–10, 67
  working with parents 9, 15, 82
  working with therapists 18–19,
   49
therapists 13
  see also occupational therapists;
   physiotherapists; speech
   therapists
timing 26, 28–9

vestibular apparatus 4, 19
visual perception 50, 72–4
vocabulary
  for movement 28
  of space and time 52–3

Walden, T. A. and Field, T. M.,
 *Pre-school Children's Social
 Competence in Production and
 Discrimination of Affective
 Expressions* 80–81
walking 25, 66